THE EXPERTS PRAISE

PRESCRIPTIONS FOR PARENTING

"Every parent, or aspiring parent, needs to read this book. This 'prescription' is for very good medicine."
—Frank A. Oski, M.D.
Chairman of Pediatrics
The Johns Hopkins University School of Medicine

• • •

"Parents, grandparents, and other child-care providers will be grateful for the practical recommendations provided here."
—Edgar O. Ledbetter, M.D.
Director, Department of Maternal, Child and Adolescent Health
American Academy of Pediatrics

• • •

"If you are frustrated by your kids' irresponsibility or bad behavior, get this book and do what it says! It shows you how to take the lead for a happier family and healthier children."
—Jean Illsley Clarke
Author of *Self-Esteem: A Family Affair, Help! for Parents,* and *Growing Up Again*

• • •

"Joyful . . . pragmatic . . . loaded with practical, effective and efficient pearls which are easy to digest and apply."
—Albert Reichert, M.D.
Clinical Professor of Pediatrics and Psychiatry and Behavior Sciences
University of Washingon

• • •

"Extraordinarily practical approach to what every set of parents faces when raising a child . . . best of all, it doesn't require a Ph.D. in Child Psychology to understand. I only wish that Dr. Meeks had had her children ten years or more earlier."

—James A. Stockman III, M.D.
Professor and Chairman, Department of Pediatrics
Northwestern University Medical School

• • •

"Eminently readable and helpful. . . . For those who want prescriptions, they are here. For those who want ideas and different approaches, they are here as well."

—Richard D. Krugman, M.D.
Vice Chairman, Department of Pediatrics
University of Colorado Health Sciences Center

• • •

"A refreshing break from tradition . . . I am very impressed with this book."

—Stephen Ludwig, M.D.
Division Chief, General Pediatrics
Children's Hospital of Philadelphia

• • •

"Readable, enjoyable, and useful. The insights gained from *Prescriptions for Parenting* will be invaluable to parents and others who care for children."

—Marianne Neifert, M.D.
Author of *Dr. Mom*
Associate Clinical Professor of Pediatrics
University of Colorado School of Medicine

• • •

"A delight to read and full of helpful information. . . . What [parents] learn will help them enjoy their children, promote their self-esteem and self-control, and prevent unnecessary struggles."

—Barry Zuckerman, M.D., F.A.A.P.
Director, Division of Behavioral and Developmental Pediatrics
Boston City Hospital

PRESCRIPTIONS FOR PARENTING

Carolyn Ann Meeks, M.D.
Illustrations by Michael J. Buschmohle

WARNER BOOKS

A Time Warner Company

W A Time Warner Company

Printed in the United States of America
First Printing: June 1990
10 9 8 7 6 5 4 3

Book design by Giorgetta Bell McRee
Cover design by Harold Nolan

Library of Congress Cataloging-in-Publication Data

Meeks, Carolyn Ann.
    Prescriptions for parenting / by Carolyn Ann Meeks.
        p.   cm.
    Includes bibliographical references.
    ISBN 0-446-39148-4
    1. Parenting—Psychological aspects.   2. Parent and child.
3. Behavior modification.   4. Self respect in children.   I. Title.
HQ755.8.M47   1990
649'.1—dc20   89-70515
                                                                          CIP

Contents

If you have tried all the techniques in this book and are still experiencing difficulties, you may need to get outside professional evaluation and support. There may be underlying causes for the behavior problems. These could be as simple as differences in temperament or family stress, or they could involve subtle or serious physical and/or psychological disabilities involving sight, hearing, word recognition and processing, speech, attention deficit disorder (ADD), autism, or childhood depression. Consult with a physician or other qualified professional for help and/or referral.

To
John, Mary, and Richard,
my three most precious jewels,
and to
Mom and Dad,
my wonderful parents

Author's Note

For the sake of simplicity I have elected to use a
single masculine or feminine pronoun to stand for a
child of either sex. Please assume that although I use
"him"/"his" in one place and "she"/"her" in another,
in each case I am referring to a child of either gender.

Acknowledgments

SPECIAL THANKS . . .

First and foremost to my children, John, Mary, and Richard, for their caring and encouragement. Also to the parents and children in my practice of medicine and in my classes, who along with my own children provided and tested the material for this book.

To Henriette Anne Klauser, Ph. D., author of *Writing on Both Sides of the Brain*, for her immense assistance in launching this project.

To my illustrator, Michael Buschmohle, who has given artistic expression to my "vision" for this book.

To Sharon Mehdi, whose assistance in writing this book was invaluable.

To Linda Crisalli and Hallie Appel, who helped me through the final revisions of the manuscript.

To Jean Clarke, Ph. D.; Michael Rothenberg, M.D.; Tona McGuire, Ph. D.; Rudolf Dreikurs, M.D.;

Jennifer James, Ph. D.; Bob Bradbury, Ph. D.; Sondra Ray; Claudia Warning, M.A.; Jerry Jampolsky, M.D.; and Dorothy Briggs, M.A.; whose teachings have influenced my beliefs and perspectives.

To Tona McGuire, Ph. D.; Marvin Ack, Ph. D.; Marianne Neifert, M.D.; Al Reichert, M.D.; and Matt Speltz, Ph. D.; for their review of the manuscript and suggestions, as well as their support.

To Brian Zeltner and John Meeks, for their Macintosh wizardry; to Gerrie Hungate, Rod Clarke, and Kristin Shirts, for their technical assistance.

To my wonderful friends and family, who were my confidants and my sounding boards, lending emotional support throughout my two-and-a-half years preparing this book.

And finally, to my editor, Joann Davis, for her astute questions, straightforward manner, and expertise.

Preface

This book is about the number one bugaboo for parents of toddlers to teens—power struggles— what causes them, how to avoid them, and how to unhook from them if you've already taken the bait. It's the kind of book you can take with you into the bathroom for a few minutes and come out a better parent. I've tried to make it upbeat, easy to understand, and accessible, so that if you only have time to look at the illustrations, you'll get the message.

And because parents who feel good about themselves and excited about their lives tend to have children who feel good about themselves, this book is also about self-esteem and how to increase it—in yourself and in your child.

In Part I, Basic Parenting, you'll discover five simple, parent-tested ways to discourage misconduct and five ways to encourage desirable behavior. You'll learn, in a few easy steps, how to handle ten of the most common behavior problems—everything from whining, messy rooms, and bedtime drama to not doing homework and fighting. You'll also develop more realistic expectations of your child for his particular age group.

Part II, Enriched Parenting, simplifies the principles you will need in order to raise kids happily. You'll learn the specifics of avoiding and "unhooking" from power struggles and how to help your child become independent and responsible for his own behavior.

In Part III, Feeling Good, you'll learn ways to increase your child's self-esteem as well as your own, how to let go of guilt, and how to have more fun as a family.

I have tried to include lots of helpful hints and reminders, or parenting "prescriptions," at the end of each chapter that you can cut out and put on your refrigerator, next to your bed, or on your desk. The more you work with these thoughts and ideas, the more they will become part of you.

Take care and enjoy!

—*Carolyn Ann Meeks, M.D.*

Introduction

A year after completing my residency in pediatrics at the University of Colorado in Denver, my beautiful son John was born. Eighteen months later, little dimpled Mary entered the world. Two years after that, Richard arrived to delight us all.

By the time my firstborn was five, I had been through two of the best pediatric training programs in the country, plus an internship in internal medicine. I secured a grant to study pediatric pharmacology, and I became a nationally recognized researcher in the field of pediatric infectious diseases. I was a frequently sought-after consultant to physicians throughout the Northwest. I was considered by many to be a "golden girl" of medicine. Professionally, it seemed, I had the world by the tail.

But as a parent of three bright, energetic, rambunctious children, I had some serious questions. Why, if I knew so much, was I unable to control their behavior? Why did my children whine and fight and refuse to put on their pajamas? Why did they say no to everything and make messes and have tantrums in the supermarket? Why did they crawl under the table in restaurants and interrupt and get dirty right after I'd gotten them clean?

My parents thought the children were unruly. The baby-sitter thought the children were unruly. Even my husband thought the children were unruly.

Why wasn't my parenting perfect? I was supposed to have all the answers, when in fact I had very few. The academic and professional challenges I faced every day were nothing compared to the challenges I faced at home in trying to figure out how to raise my own children.

The turning point for me, my children, and my career came one spring day in 1980 when I was given a piece of advice that answered one of my problems.

John's whining, which I thought should have ended with the "two's," had finally gotten the best of me. Nothing I tried had any effect at all, except perhaps to increase the problem. I was frantic. The advice provided a simple recipe for how to cure what had become an incredibly annoying childhood behavior. I followed the formula, and within three days my child had stopped whining completely! I was so impressed by the results that I immediately applied for admission to a Ph.D. program in child psychology.

During the next few years, I was like a sponge. I studied behavioral pediatrics, behavioral medicine, family therapy, crisis intervention, parenting, and self-esteem therapy. I wanted to learn everything I could about how to be a more effective parent, and I wanted to pass on what I had learned to the parents of my patients.

One of the first things I realized was that there was a conflict between wanting to control my children and wanting them to grow up to be independent thinking, self-reliant, creative individuals.

It became clear that I was going to have to give up one or the other. I decided to give up my need to control.

I discovered that if I thought of myself as a *caring coach* instead of a controlling parent, I could transform my own thinking as well as the behavior of my children. A caring coach knows how to encourage his players as well as how to blow the whistle and establish limits. In the years that followed, as I taught workshops on parenting and self-esteem for families, I found that enhancing the self-esteem of both the parent and child had a dramatic and positive impact on the child's behavior. In 1984, I opened the Parent Resource Institute in Seattle, a counseling center for parents who "want to run away."

John, Mary, and Richard, who are now fourteen, twelve, and ten, are delightful joy-filled examples of how well the concept of parental guidance rather than parental control works. Every technique and bit of insight that appears in this book is something that has worked with my own children or with my patients and clients. Because of these techniques, I can laugh more often and resolve differences more readily than ever before.

Parenting wasn't meant to be a *constant* battle, and with the techniques and tips in this book, it may never be that again!

Part I • BASIC PARENTING

1 • It Takes Two to Make a Power Struggle

If you've never found yourself nose-to-nose with a screaming, belligerent, unyielding child whose stubborn refusal to do things *your* way has turned you into a screaming, belligerent, unyielding adult, then pat yourself on the back and find something else to do with your time.

But if either of the following incidents sounds the least bit familiar, join the crowd. This is the book for you.

In fact, it may be the only book on parenting you'll ever need to read.

This is a book for exasperated parents. Kind, tender-hearted, caring parents who by some queer quirk of fate find themselves sharing home and hearth with offspring who vacillate between being loving, adorable moppets and throwbacks to Attila the Hun.

Take Christopher, for example. He's a bright, sensitive, happy-faced four-year-old who can turn a household upside down and his parents inside out when he wants his own way, which is a lot of the time. He knows exactly how to engage his parents in a power struggle that rivals the Battle of Gettysburg for explosive intensity. Mealtime is a favorite of his for this—mainly because he has everyone's attention and he knows how important it is to his parents that he eat well-balanced meals.

A recent incident began innocently enough when Christopher's dad asked him to stop playing with his meat loaf and start eating it.

"I don't like it," he said. "It's got ONIONS in it."

"I took all the onions out of your meat loaf," said Dad, who had spent several minutes in the kitchen doing just that.

"No you didn't, here's one," Christopher answered, pointing out a microscopic sliver of what may at one time have been part of an onion.

"Well, maybe I missed one. Just put it on the edge of the plate and eat the rest of the meat loaf."

"No!" said Christopher, as he got down from his chair.

"Yes!" said Dad, his voice and temper rising. "Get back up there and eat that meat loaf!"

"No!" Christopher shouted without budging. "IT SMELLS LIKE ONIONS AND I HATE IT!"

At that point, Dad picked up a screaming, kicking Christopher, plunked him down solidly on the chair and bellowed in his son's face, "WE HAD MEAT LOAF LAST WEEK AND YOU ATE IT, SO EAT IT NOW!"

"I WON'T AND YOU CAN'T MAKE ME!" Christopher shrieked.

"I CAN AND I WILL!" screamed Dad, with the veins on his forehead popping out ominously.

The issue, at that point, was neither the dreaded meat loaf nor whether Christopher ate it. It was whether a four-year-old attempting to assert his independence was going to get the best of a thirty-six-year-old man attempting to assert his control. Father and son both ended up feeling angry, exhausted, and guilty. There was no "winner."

Then there's the case of Jennifer. Her parent-baiting technique was more subtle, but just as effective.

Like most average eleven-year-olds, Jennifer is not known for her tidiness. For her, a made bed consists of a blanket pulled over a two-foot-high pile of stuffed animals, dirty clothes, school books, and decaying foodstuffs.

"Go upstairs and clean that room of yours, young lady," Jennifer's mom said one day, after being unable to open her daughter's door because of the debris blocking it.

"CLEAN MY ROOM?" Jennifer yelped with genuine astonishment. "I just cleaned my room last week! How come I'm the only kid who has to work when she gets home from school? Everybody else gets to go out and play. But not me! I have to work, work, work. I bet you had kids just so you'd have somebody to do the work!"

"Listen here, little Miss Snippit, I'll have you know that when I was your age I was taking care of four younger brothers and sisters, doing ALL the housework, milking the cows, taking in ironing, walking twenty-four miles to and from school in the snow. . . ." You know the rest. Jennifer had pushed her mom's button and the fight was on.

Here again, the original issue of the room was lost in chaos and conflict.

These are the kinds of power struggles that go on at one time or another in nearly every home that is shared by a child and a parent, the kind of energy-sapping, esteem-deadening power struggles that *can* be prevented.

DISAGREEMENT IS NORMAL

All parent-child relationships entail some conflict. It's been said, "Love breeds conflict." As long as you have two thinking individuals you will have different opinions, and that's good. Without diversity of interests, creative individuality, and strength of convictions, we'd be as boring as unsalted popcorn.

It is very important to acknowledge conflict and to deal with it as it comes up. Conflict can be dealt with in a constructive or destructive manner.

Destructive struggle shreds self-esteem, inhibits personal growth, and limits fulfillment of one's potential. Destructive struggle is also frequently noisy, exhausting, and embarrassing (especially if it takes place in the express line at Safeway, while the in-laws are visiting, or in front of the new minister).

Constructive resolution promotes personal growth and allows the child *and* the parent to reach their full potential. The good news is that it is not only possible to achieve, it's really quite easy with the help of the new strategies you will learn in this book.

Disagreement is normal.

IS FIGHTING WITH YOUR CHILD REALLY NECESSARY?

Full-scale battles between parents and children tend to be destructive and are usually unnecessary. If you must battle, choose your battles wisely. Concentrate on what is really important—i.e., major issues. Major issues might include honesty, integrity, and communication. They will vary according to your own value system. Ask yourself how important a situation is. In the cases cited above, Jennifer is not going to be physically or psychologically damaged from living in preadolescent squalor a few more days. And Christopher will grow up healthy and strong even if he doesn't eat his meat loaf one night. Pick battles you can win—e.g., you will not win battles over food. Short of becoming abusive, you will not be able to force your child to eat. These issues may need to be addressed, but not with all-out war.

Is fighting with your child really necessary?

WHY DO PARENTS *HATE* BEING CHALLENGED BY THEIR CHILDREN?

So why then do these day-to-day issues seem so very important, so worth fighting about?

Intense anger or rage comes from a feeling of powerlessness. Many of us grew up believing that good parents by definition are always in control of their children's actions or behavior. So when a child "pushes the limits," the parent may feel somewhat incompetent and inadequate. To compensate for the feeling, a parent may resort to monsterlike outrage. Try to remember that a challenge from your child does not mean that you are a failure as a parent.

Why do parents hate being challenged by their children?

IT TAKES TWO TO MAKE A POWER STRUGGLE

Just as there have to be opponents before there can be a war, there has to be more than one participant in a power struggle. If one person stops pushing or pulling and steps aside, there is nothing for the other to struggle against.

This book will give you ways to work with your child rather than against him—toward constructive resolution of the normal conflicts that arise in every home.

In the beginning, it may take a bit of determination not to become a four-year-old right along with your four-year-old—or not to become as adolescent as your adolescent. But with awareness and the techniques in this book, which have proven successful with hundreds of families, including my own, soon power struggles will be a thing of the past.

Remember, it takes two to make a power struggle.

Remember, it takes two to make a power struggle.

REMEMBER—

- Disagreement is normal
- There are alternatives to fighting
- Conflict is an opportunity for positive change and understanding
- It takes two to make a power struggle

REMEMBER...

✓ DISAGREEMENT IS NORMAL

✓ THERE ARE ALTERNATIVES TO FIGHTING

✓ CONFLICT IS AN OPPORTUNITY FOR POSITIVE CHANGE & UNDERSTANDING

✓ IT TAKES TWO TO MAKE A POWER STRUGGLE

Dispense ad lib _____ Carolyn Ann Meeks _____ M.D.

2 • Catch 'Em Being Good

The best way to cure the power-struggle routine is to avoid it in the first place—by encouraging positive, acceptable behavior and discouraging negative, unacceptable behavior.

Sounds easy, right? And it is.

Many of us tend to make parenting a lot more complicated than it needs to be. For starters, I recommend that you:

Treat your kids like company.

If you want your children to treat you with respect and consideration, treat them with the same respect and consideration you would show to a guest! We get back what we give, so be sure that what you give to your children is what you want in return.

17

**Treat your kids
like company.**

For example, you would never yell at your guests or order them around. If you needed help or cooperation you would speak to them politely with words like "please" and "thank you."

Look for the best and that's usually what you'll find.

A remarkable example of this rule in action occurred several years ago in an area of Seattle known for its high crime rate. An elderly woman was walking down the street when a young man came up from behind and attempted to grab her purse.

The woman held tightly to her purse, swung around and, looking her accoster straight in the eye, she yelled, "Young man, you're *better* than this!" The would-be mugger stared at her for a few seconds, then turned around and walked away. That brave lady had looked for the best and found it. I don't recommend trying this with muggers, but I do recommend trying it with your child: "You know you can act better than that."

**Look for the best and that's usually
what you'll find.**

See misbehavior as the exception,
not the rule.

FIVE WAYS TO ENCOURAGE DESIRED BEHAVIOR

---

1. Catch 'em being good.

Children often repeat behavior that draws attention. That fact may sound simple, yet often we tend to overlook those times when our child does what we ask, is generous with his toys, picks up after himself, chews and actually swallows his green beans, does his homework, plays quietly, goes to bed without a fuss. Instead, we put all our attention and energy into those times he doesn't.

When your child does something you want to see more of, notice it! Acknowledge his actions directly! With a younger child, this can be through hugs, pats, smiles, oohs and aahs. Talk about his behavior to others. Children have radar-like reception when you're talking about them; let them overhear a conversation in which the merits of their behavior are being enthusiastically acknowledged.

Catch 'em being good.

2. Acknowledge improvement.

The next time your child improves his behavior—e.g., upgrades his schoolwork from a D to a C, gets up earlier in the morning, or brushes his teeth better—talk about it. Notice the smallest effort, even if you know your child can do better. "I want you to know I *do* notice that you are trying harder." If the improvement is dramatic, you might say, "Now, that's improvement!" When you acknowledge any improvement it reinforces your child's willingness to try again.

Acknowledge improvement.

3. Use positive reinforcers.

Consider the rewards listed below that your child likes most and use them as reinforcers for positive behavior:

• For a child under ten, consider the time-honored star chart. First-grade teachers of the world have used this for eons, because it works. Kids love to amass stars! Gold stars for truly spectacular performance. Blue for great. Green for pretty darn good. Red for "Wow, you've improved!" Be creative and be generous!

• For a child over the age of ten, add privileges. This technique can produce miracles. Children are so conditioned to having things taken away for misbehavior that we get their immediate attention when we add privileges for good behavior—staying up later, special outings and adventures where friends can come along, a boost in allowance. Make it something you know your child will especially appreciate.

Use positive reinforcers.

Look over this list and check off the rewards that are the most appropriate for your child. Better yet, go over this list with your child to select possible rewards for improved behavior. Often the best reward is one-on-one time with you, the parent.

REWARDS AND ENCOURAGEMENTS

SPECIAL TIME WITH MOM OR DAD

- ☐ Reading aloud
- ☐ Card games
- ☐ Board games
- ☐ Looking through family photos
- ☐ Throwing or kicking a ball around

ENTERTAINMENT

- ☐ TV
- ☐ Movies
- ☐ Videos
- ☐ Video games
- ☐ Tapes

ARTS AND CRAFTS

- ☐ Painting
- ☐ Play Dough
- ☐ Drawing

SOCIAL ACTIVITIES

- ☐ Having a friend over for the day
- ☐ Hugs or kisses
- ☐ Baking cookies
- ☐ Having friends sleep over

LESSONS

- ☐ Piano
- ☐ Dance
- ☐ Art
- ☐ Guitar

NEW CLOTHES

- ☐ Shorts
- ☐ Shoes
- ☐ Bathing suit
- ☐ Hat

EDIBLES AND CHEWABLES

- ☐ Sugarless gum
- ☐ Fruit
- ☐ Special snack (Granola, trail mix)

OUTINGS

- ☐ Trip to the library
- ☐ Trip to playground
- ☐ Camping
- ☐ Fishing trip
- ☐ Zoo
- ☐ Ice cream outing
- ☐ Visit to grandparents

4. Offer choices.

Whenever possible, give your child a choice rather than a command. Instead of saying, "Be quiet!" say, "You can stay here and play quietly, or you can go outside and make all the noise you want." Instead of saying, "Put on your jacket," say, "Would you like a red jacket or a green jacket?"

Whenever possible offer your child choices.

5. Use distraction.

If you want a younger child to put on a seat belt, go potty, put on a pajama top, or any other maneuver, offer a distraction. Instead of saying, "Do you want to put on your seat belt?" ask, "Do you want to hear a story about Sessie the Dog while I put on your seat belt?" (Notice the question here is whether or not he wants the story, not whether or not he is going to have you put on his seat belt.)

Use distraction.

You can almost always detour your child away from mischievous behavior by being playful with him or by telling a story (especially if it includes himself and a fuzzy animal). If you're not feeling creative, try the story below.

SESSIE THE DOG

Nathan, do you want to hear a story about Sessie the dog? Well, once there was a dog named Sessie and there was a little boy named Nathan, and one day Nathan went to visit his grandmother. Sessie the dog kept jumping up and down and barking! Well, Grandma told Sessie, "Don't, Sessie, don't!" and Nathan, who was hardly old enough to speak, shouted, "DOWN, Sessie, DOWN!"

FIVE WAYS TO DISCOURAGE UNACCEPTABLE BEHAVIOR

No matter how diligent you are at complimenting and reinforcing good behavior, there will be times—probably lots of them—when inappropriate or undesirable behavior becomes a concern. It's a normal child's job to see just how much he can get away with. It's your job to set the limits.

Here are some guidelines for discouraging unacceptable behavior should it come up:

1. Ignore attention-getting nondestructive misbehavior.

In younger children, pouting and excessive arguing and mildly questionable language are examples of behavior you might want to overlook. If a child uses the word "penis" and sees that it gets a rousing response from parents, siblings, and visitors, he will probably use it every chance he gets. If, however, parents and visitors ignore it (you can't count on siblings for this), he's likely to drop it as ineffective. Tantrums can also be attention-getting devices. When they are, ignore the uproar and follow with a time-out. (A time-out is a period of quiet that lasts until your child is ready to behave.)

2. Express your anger briefly. Stop. Wait for your words to sink in.

It is normal for you to feel anger toward your child at times. Sometimes the most effective way to deal with inappropriate behavior is a sharp "NO!" or "STOP!" or "I'm angry with you!" Explain briefly and to the point why you are angry. Do not resort to insults or name-calling. Always follow the outburst with a pause to allow yourself to "put it into neutral" and regain your composure. A pause has much more impact than ranting and raving, which can diminish your credibility with your child. And finally, the pause also serves to give your child the opportunity for your message to sink in. Follow the pause with appropriate consequences.

Note: If you have a problem controlling your anger, simply give your child a time-out and take a time-out yourself.

Ignore attention-getting nondestructive misbehavior.

Express your anger briefly. Stop. Wait for your words to sink in.

3. Call a time-out.

When behavior such as rudeness, trampling the flower beds, playing in the fireplace, or hitting and throwing things around occurs, give a time-out. Assume your child wants to behave. For a child who is "losing it," time-out can be a time for the child to get himself back under control. As a general rule, give one minute per year of age. After that, your child will forget what the whole thing was about. (A two-year-old has a two-minute attention span; a four-year-old, a four-minute attention span; and so on.) Use a minute timer. If your child is not ready to cooperate, reset the timer. Younger children hate boredom. So the time-out should be in a place devoid of toys or diversions —on the couch, on a stairway, in a room where there is nothing appealing to play with or nothing to do. (See chapter 6, number 3.)

Important: Forget the idea of three admonitions or warnings.* By the third one you'll be ready to explode. If you have made a rule clear to your child, give a time-out with the first offense. If a child doesn't remember the rule, he'll learn it quickly.

---

*Some parents will repeatedly admonish their child not to do something—e.g., "Don't go near the plant" . . . then later, "I told you not to go near the plant."

Call a time-out
for misbehavior.

4. Withdraw privileges.

With a child over ten, for an offense such as not doing homework or chores, instead of giving a time-out, withdraw privileges. Taking away whatever privileges your child is most attached to—e.g., TV time, allowance, excursions, stereo, phone time—is generally what will have the most profound effect.

Withdraw privileges.

5. Allow natural consequences to take place.

Allowing your child to face the natural consequences of behavior that doesn't directly impact you can often be the best approach. For instance, if your child doesn't do his homework, he will have to face the consequences the next day in class. If he swiped a Snickers from the corner market,

IF YOUR CHILD DOESN'T DO HIS HOMEWORK, LET HIM FACE THE MUSIC WITH HIS TEACHER...

JOEL, PLEASE TELL US WHAT YOU LEARNED FROM YOUR HOMEWORK ASSIGNMENT

Allow natural consequences to take place.

return him and the candy wrapper to the store and let him face the music with the manager. (See chapter 7, number 5.)

ABOUT SPANKING

Is it O.K. to use spanking to discourage inappropriate behavior?

Having learned all of the techniques in this book and realizing how effective they are, I do not recommend spanking as an approach to discipline. (Remember, discipline means to teach, not to punish.) An exception to the above might be an occasional swat to discourage very dangerous behavior, such as running into the street, sticking a finger into a light socket, reaching for a hot iron, or throwing a brick at another child.

In my experience there are many reasons to avoid spanking:

- It's too easy to "lose it" and hit too hard or too much.
- Other techniques work better than spanking in the long run and equally well in the short run.

There are rare occasions when nothing works. In these cases remember, sometimes it's O.K. to lose some points as long as you win the game.

- Stubborn children will only become more stubborn with spanking.
- When a child is really angry and out of control, spanking tends to "wind up" rather than "wind down."

Remember, I do not recommend spanking. However, if you must use spanking, it is important to restrict it as follows:

- *Do not* spank with objects such as a wooden spoon, switch, or belt. Use the flat of the hand only.
- *Do not* use more than three swats. If your child does not seem to be responding, DO NOT *escalate*; it may break your child's spirit, and you'll be ashamed of yourself later.
- *Do not* spank any part of the body except the buttocks or thighs. The only exception to this could be a light swat on the back of the hand.
- *Never* shake a child. Shaking can result in damage to the brain, eyes, or other organs.
- Be sure to tell the child that what he did was very dangerous and that you were afraid he'd hurt himself or others very badly, if this is the case.

IF YOU HAVE A PROBLEM WITH CONTROLLING ANGER, DO NOT SPANK A CHILD UNDER ANY CIRCUMSTANCES.

FIVE WAYS TO ENCOURAGE DESIRED BEHAVIOR

- Catch 'em being good
- Acknowledge improvement
- Use positive reinforcements
- Offer choices
- Use distraction

 FIVE WAYS TO ENCOURAGE DESIRED BEHAVIOR

- ✓ CATCH 'EM BEING GOOD
- ✓ ACKNOWLEDGE IMPROVEMENT
- ✓ USE POSITIVE REINFORCERS
- ✓ OFFER CHOICE
- ✓ USE DISTRACTION

 Dispense ad lib _____ *Carolyn Ann Meeks* _____ M.D.

FIVE WAYS TO DISCOURAGE UNACCEPTABLE BEHAVIOR

- Ignore attention-getting behavior
- Express your anger briefly . . . wait for your words to sink in
- Take time-out for misbehavior
- Withdraw privileges
- Allow natural consequences to take place

 FIVE WAYS TO DISCOURAGE UNACCEPTABLE BEHAVIOR

✓ IGNORE ATTENTION-GETTING BEHAVIOR

✓ EXPRESS YOUR ANGER BRIEFLY...WAIT FOR YOUR WORDS TO SINK IN

✓ TAKE TIME-OUT FOR MISBEHAVIOR

✓ WITHDRAW PRIVILEGES

✓ ALLOW NATURAL CONSEQUENCES TO TAKE PLACE

 Dispense ad lib _____ Carolyn Ann Meeks _____ M.D.

3 • Ten Common Problems and How to Solve Them

Many of us grew up in homes with well-meaning parents who believed it was their role to make their kids obey. Authoritarian control was the name of the game. That was how our parents were raised, and they had no other role model. Sometimes the approach worked, but a lot of times it created problems that we grown-up kids are still dealing with.

My way and the way of other contemporary child rearing experts of bringing up children stresses teaching and guidance instead of control and punishment. And for parents who can make the internal shift from trying to control their children to accepting their role as teacher and guide, the results can be remarkable.

But because most of us don't have any role models for this new approach, we need help.

FIVE KEYS TO SUCCESS

Here are five sure-fire ways of communicating with your child without resorting to the phrase, "You'll do it because I said so!"

1. Don't respond to uproar.

No matter what the issue is—you want your child to do one thing and he wants to do another—expect initial resistance in the form of uproar. Most adults enter parenthood without ever knowing what uproar is. Uproar is a smoke screen that children create to distract you from your task in setting limits. It comes in different forms—for example, noise: "Waah"; or blaming: "You're mean"; or excuses: "I'm tired"; or complaining: "How come John doesn't have to empty the trash?" Your job is to *ignore the uproar, no matter what form it takes*.

Don't respond to uproar.

2. Restate your expectations or concerns.

Be ready to repeat a directive. For instance, "I expect you to take the trash out now." Whine . . . complain . . . whine. "I expect you to take the trash out now." Don't worry about sounding like a broken record. Frequently, that's what it takes for your child to eventually understand that you do, indeed, expect him to take out the trash now.

Restate your expectations or concerns.

3. Offer the "When . . . then" incentive.

Here's a concept that will make parenting more fun. Instead of threatening your child, offer a positive incentive: "When you've taken out the trash, then we can make popcorn"; "When you've cleaned your room, then we'll go to the mall"; "When your homework is done, then you can go out and play."

WHEN YOU TAKE THE TRASH OUT, THEN WE'LL MAKE POPCORN!

Offer the "When . . . then" incentive.

4. Use the magic word "nevertheless."

After listening to your child's feelings and considering his perspective and requests, determine what is best for both of you and set a bottom-line limit with the magic word "nevertheless": "I realize it's cold outside; nevertheless, I want you to take the trash out now." "I know you want to ride your bike; nevertheless, you will have to clean up your mess first!" I'm not sure exactly what makes this word so powerful and effective, but countless parents have thanked me for it.

Use the
magic word
"nevertheless."

5. Think ahead: plan together for a mutually "happy" resolution.

This is one of the most important points in this entire book. If you have a problem with your child, involve him in the resolution. Assume that your child wants to behave in ways he can be proud of. At a time when you are both calm, sit down and talk with your child. Ask him, for example, "Jeremy, how can we make chore time a happy time for both of us?" Acknowledge your child's ideas and try his ideas if at all possible. Any time a child becomes involved in the solution of a problem, he is more apt to embrace it. (See chapter 7, number 4.)

Think ahead: plan together for a mutually "happy" resolution.

THE TEN PROBLEMS AND HOW TO RESOLVE THEM

Here are some tips for handling those situations when your wondrous, delightful, fun-filled children have tried your patience and sanity to their very limits with decidedly undelightful behavior.

Fighting

Willie and Wailin' were the nicknames given to the six- and eight-year-old sons of one of my friends. The two children were always fighting over something, and their mom was constantly trying to unravel the situation, assess the damage, and place the blame. It was time-consuming, tiresome, and counterproductive to peaceful coexistence. And it had to stop.

"Willie hit me!" Wailin' wailed as he staggered into the kitchen clutching his side, apparently in great pain.

"WILLIE, GET DOWN HERE THIS MINUTE!" roared Mom from the bottom of the stairs.

"What's the matter, Mom?" asked an innocent-faced Willie from the landing.

"What did you do to your brother?"

"Nothin'."

"He said you hit him."

"Honest, Mom, I didn't do anything!"

Fighting

"You did, too," piped up Wailin'. "You hit me in the side [sob, sob, sob, sob]!"

"I just pushed him to get him away from my cars."

"He wouldn't let me play with the cars," Wailin' wailed.

"You crybaby," Willie said. "Crybaby, crybaby!"

"Stop being mean, Willie!" shouted Mom.

"I am not a crybaby [sob, sob]."

At this point, Mom threw up her hands. "I can't take it any more! You two have got to stop this fighting! Willie, go to your room right now!"

Sometimes when children fight, it is to get your attention. When you jump in, you're feeding into it.

RESOLUTION:

1. Ignore the uproar and high drama.
2. State your expectations—"I expect you two to settle your differences without hitting."
3. Send the children to separate rooms to cool off.
4. Use the "When . . . then" incentive: "When you're ready to settle your argument without hitting, then you can come out of your room."
5. Involve your children in establishing ground rules about fair fighting—e.g., no hitting, no name calling. Allow your children to come up with consequences for violations. My own children created

a system in which they pay each other 10 cents for name calling. Try using your children's ideas first, with your assistance, if necessary, for enforcement. (See chapter 12, number 2.)

Note: In this example, Mom feels her role is to be a judge and is identifying with the victimized child. Mom needs to realize it takes two to make a fight. The kids are engaged in a victim/persecutor dance and Mom is playing rescuer. As soon as Mom gets involved she has made the judgment that her children are incapable of handling the situation themselves. By stepping back or refusing to become embroiled in the dispute, Mom is actually empowering her children to resolve their differences themselves.

Talking Back

"Don't you talk back to me, or you'll go straight to your room." Dad bristles at his four-year-old son Jeremy, who has just told his father he isn't going to pick up the mess he's made on the floor.

"I'll talk back if I want to. You can't stop me!" says Jeremy, with his feet apart and hands on hips.

"Oh yes I can!" says Dad, picking up his son, putting him in his room, and closing the door. Jeremy pulls and tugs on the door, trying to get out, as Dad holds it closed.

"You skunk-brain dirt catcher!" Jeremy yells from behind the door. "You are a stupid dummy! You messy slug!" The four-year-old kicks the door hard with his foot.

"You watch your tongue, Mister Smartmouth!" Dad yells back.

"You watch YOURS!" Jeremy says as he flings his body against the door.

Dad feels his anger rising out of control.

RESOLUTION:

1. Step back—do not engage in the uproar. *Do not match your child's anger.* Remind your child that you care about him and that his behavior is inappropriate. Often when a child says he hates you or calls you names, he's acting out the fact that he feels unlovable. You might want to say, "I love you; I don't like your behavior." You could also say, "Wow! That's a pretty yukky name you thought up! How about we see if a messy slug can help clean up a messy floor?" using humor to end the confrontation.

Talking Back

2. If your child calls you a name identify his feelings: "You're angry."
3. State your expectations: "You can say you're angry without name calling."
4. Take a time-out. Tell your child, "Your time-out is over when you can behave in a way you can be proud of." If you overreact, give yourself a time-out to cool off. Remove yourself physically from the child. Don't go back until you are under control. (It would be better for the father to let the whole thing drop and never readdress the problem than to get back in there when he's feeling out of control. Discipline means to teach and guide; it doesn't mean to overpower. What has helped me—and hundreds of other parents—to maintain composure is to say to myself, "I'm the adult, he's the child.")
5. After both parent and child have cooled off, the parent could sit down with the child and say, "Let's talk about this. We need to set up some ground rules about not talking back."

Whining

Only someone who has lived in the same household with a whining child can truly appreciate the degree of irritation one small, plaintive voice can create in an otherwise gentle, loving parent.

"Can't I have a snack, pleeeeeese," seven-year-old Tina whines. "C'mon, Mom, just one more, pleeeeeese."

"For heaven's sake, stop that whining," Mom says.

"I will if you give me a snack, pleeeeeese," Tina whines.

Whining

"Didn't you hear me? Stop whining!"

Tina can tell from the look on her mother's face that it's time to regroup. She goes into the family room and returns thirty seconds later with her Cuddly-Kathy doll. "Pleeeeeese, Mom, can Kathy have a snack?" Tina whines.

Mom's eyes roll to the back of her head.

A whining child is often the result of the "tender-hearted-parent syndrome." She is the child of a parent who always puts the child's needs and wants first, who nearly always gives in to the whining. Consequently the child knows that whining is an effective way to get what she wants.

RESOLUTION:

1. Ignore the whining. Children do annoying things to get their parents' attention. If you acknowledge the whining, you're reinforcing it.
2. Never grant any request asked for while whining. Let your child know that his request is not even open to discussion while he's whining.
3. Tell your child to ask you again later in a normal voice.
4. Use the "When . . . then" incentive: "When you're ready to talk in a normal voice, then we can look into getting a snack."

Note: When the child addresses you later in a normal voice, be sure to acknowledge and reward her in some way—e.g., a hug or a pat or a snack if appropriate.

Interrupting

I have a friend with whom I have not had an uninterrupted conversation since her son, Michael, turned two. Michael is going to be nine soon and he still waits until his mother is on the phone or in deep conversation with a visitor to ask if he can have $5 for the movies, spend the night with Jason even though it's a school night, buy a new pair of Reeboks, or whatever.

Michael knows, from years of experience, that his kind-hearted, peace-loving mother is much more apt to give in to him if he makes his requests in front of her friends or while she's on the phone with them.

As a toddler, Michael required a lot of attention and reassurance. When his mom and dad were talking to each other, or to someone else, that meant they weren't paying attention to him. So he'd say or do something to change the focus. Like clutch his crotch and say, "Potty!" whether he had to go or not. Or he'd tug on his mom's arm—and tug and tug and tug. Or wrap his chubby little arms around his dad's leg—and pull and pull and pull.

As he became more verbal, he would simply ask whatever highly irrelevant question came to his mind whenever he happened upon a conversation taking place that didn't include him. And because Mom and Dad always stopped midsentence and gave him their full attention, even if just to tell him to stop interrupting, he kept it up.

But after six and a half years, Mom and Dad are tired of the interruptions and embarrassed by them.

Interrupting

RESOLUTION:

Parents need to learn to have respect for themselves and their needs, which includes their right to have uninterrupted conversations with their friends and spouse. In turn, children will learn to have respect and consideration for others.

1. Sit down with your child and explain to him that it is important for you to have adult time, or special time, that's just for you. Discuss the concepts of self-respect and mutual respect. Make your expectations clear. Ask your child for his ideas about rewards for improvement or consequences for violations of the ground rules.
2. Do not grant *any* requests made while you are on the phone.
3. If you are dealing with a younger child who interrupts, stop the conversation and give him a time-out immediately.
4. At the same time, you need to set realistic expectations regarding your child's needs as well as your own. For example, if you've been on the phone for an hour and your child needs bus money to get to soccer practice, it is unrealistic to expect him not to interrupt you at some point as the time gets later and later. If it's a long conversation by necessity, perhaps you can stop every fifteen minutes to survey the home front.

Inappropriate Dress

"There's no way I'm going to let you go to school looking like that!" Amy's mom tells her thirteen-year-old daughter as she flies through the kitchen one Monday morning.

"What's wrong with the way I look?" Amy asks incredulously.

"Well, for starters, the black nail polish. And your skirt is so short I can see your belly button. And the thing you're wearing on top looks like something you wear UNDER your clothes, not in place of them."

"Mom! All the girls dress like this. This isn't the olden days you know. We don't have to dress like 'Little House on the Prairie,' like when you were in school."

"I don't care what all the girls are wearing, you're not going to school like that! And wash all that makeup off your face while you're at it. You're too young to be wearing all that stuff."

"Well, I might as well just die right now then," Amy yells, "because my life is ruined! I might as well be a nun or something. I'll never have any friends and everybody's going to laugh at me. You've ruined my life!"

The sobbing thirteen-year-old runs up the stairs and slams the door to her room, leaving Mom to ponder the joys of budding adolescence.

RESOLUTION:

Remember, you're here to guide and teach your child. There's often a fine line between controlling and caring concern. Try to be clear in your own mind which you are expressing.

Inappropriate Dress

Here is my recommended approach:

1. State your expectations: "I expect you to dress more appropriately, and I want you to change your outfit."
2. Ignore any ensuing uproar.
3. Restate your expectations: "I understand you're angry with me; nevertheless, you will have to change before you go to school."
4. For an older child, openly and honestly discuss your values regarding sexually provocative ways of dressing. Set a bottom line for what is acceptable and then allow her to make her own choices within those boundaries. With a younger child, try to be flexible as she is developing her taste and style; only interfere if her choices are very inappropriate for the occasion or the weather.

Not Doing Homework

Tuesday evening:
   "No TV until you've finished your homework, Todd," said Mom.
   "I didn't have any homework today," the eleven-year-old answered.
   "You didn't? That's two days in a row with no homework. What's going on at school?"
   "We do everything in class."
Wednesday evening:
   "No TV until you've finished your homework, Todd."

Not Doing Homework

"I finished before you got home."

Thursday evening:

"No TV until you've finished your homework, Todd."

"It's all done, Mom."

And on it goes.

Two weeks later, report cards come out and Todd's grades have fallen dramatically. The reason given: "Does not turn in homework assignments."

There are three problems here—the child lying, the parent who is out of touch, and the child not doing his homework.

RESOLUTIONS:

1. Regarding the child lying: Don't interrogate or cross-examine. Often this only produces further lying. Do sit down with your child and ask, "What's going on with you here?" "What do *you* plan to do about it?" State your expectations: "I expect that when you say your homework is done, it really is. I've lost my trust in your word on the subject of homework, and you're going to have to earn it back."

2. Regarding parental detachment: Spend time with your child and show an interest in what he is studying at school. Try to make homework more fun for him.

3. Regarding not doing homework: withdraw privileges initially. After you've seen improvement use "When . . . then" incentives: "When you show me that you have completed your homework, then you can watch TV." "When your homework is done, then you can go out and play."

4. It is important to encourage your child's independence before the age of ten. Involve him in establishing a workable schedule to do his homework. Then, as he approaches the teen years, you can begin to back off and let him handle his school responsibilities himself. If he is doing satisfactory work, then he should be allowed to develop his own routine. It really doesn't matter if he does his homework before or after he plays, as long as it gets done.

Bedtime Drama

"It's nine o'clock, son, time for bed," Dad says to Mark.

"C'mon, Dad, can't I just watch the beginning of *Monsters from Another Planet*?" begs the eight-year-old.

"Mark, we go through this every night. You know that nine o'clock is your bedtime, so get on in there right now. I'll come in and say good night in a minute."

"Well, can I just pick up my stuff?" Mark asks, with his eyes glued to the TV.

"Pick up your stuff, but do it fast!" Dad says, realizing he's being had.

Mark moves at the pace of an arthritic turtle.

"Mark, I know what you're doing—now, get to bed!" Dad says, turning up his volume.

"I'm going, I'm going," Mark says as he "accidentally" drops all the things he has just picked up, necessitating a further delay while he gathers them again.

Bedtime Drama

"MARK, GET IN YOUR ROOM THIS INSTANT!" Dad yells.

"You're always telling me to pick up my stuff, and then when I try to do it you yell at me!" Mark answers indignantly, his eyes still on the TV.

"MOVE IT!" Dad bellows.

Mark saunters off to his room.

RESOLUTION:

1. Ignore the uproar, i.e. dawdling, often an attention-getting maneuver.
2. State your expectations: "I expect you to go to bed at nine o'clock without using delaying tactics."
3. Use the "When . . . then" incentive: "When you're ready for bed, then you can watch TV or play until nine o'clock." If your child dawdles, let it cut into his playtime, not your relaxation time.
4. Try having a separate bedtime routine that includes a half hour to wind down before bed with stories, cuddles, or special relaxation time with parents. This is a good time to ask him about his day.
5. Think ahead. Involve your child in creating consequences. For example, if the child is fifteen minutes late to bed on Tuesday, he has to go to bed fifteen minutes earlier on Wednesday. Until there is noticeable improvement, you may want to have your child get ready for bed right after dinner.
6. If you have a problem with a child who pops up and down after being put to bed, set the clear limit of only one time out of the room allowed.

Note: Realize that children have variable needs for sleep. For some children bedtime wakefulness is an indication that their daytime sleep (i.e., sleeping-in late in the morning and/or afternoon nap) needs to be limited.

Poor Eating Habits

Kevin was ten years old and only ate foods whose main ingredients were sugar, chemicals, and grease.

It wasn't that his parents didn't try. Week after week they prepared tasty, appealing meals and had healthful snacks on hand. They talked to their son about the importance of balanced eating. But it was to no avail.

Kevin simply refused to eat anything that looked as if it might have a vegetable lurking somewhere in it, wasn't fried, didn't come in a bun, or didn't have pepperoni on it.

He used his allowance to buy candy bars and Twinkies. He drank Coke instead of milk.

His health-conscious parents were frantic.

RESOLUTION:

1. Get rid of all junk food in your house, including your own. If any adult in the house must have junk food, ask him or her to keep it at work or elsewhere.

Poor Eating Habits

2. State your concerns. "I'm concerned about your health. My hope is that you will choose to eat a well-balanced diet and save the junk food for now and then."
3. Don't supply your child with an unlimited budget for candy and soft drinks. You could opt to restrict the use of his allowance for junk food.
4. As much as possible, plan menus within your child's taste and preferences. There is no reason to expect him to like everything. Introduce new foods when he is particularly hungry.
5. Ask your pediatrician or family doctor to address the issue with your child. Sometimes input from an expert can have a positive impact on your child's perspective.

Note: Make sure you don't use food issues as a primary battleground. While you can control the food choices that are available to your child, you cannot force him to eat.

Messy Room

Mindi has the neatest closet and bureau drawers of any eleven-year-old girl on her block. The reason they're so neat is because every stitch of apparel Mindi owns is on the floor, draped over the chair, hanging from the lamp, piled on the bed, or balled up under it.

Mixed in with the jumble of clothing are bowls and plates of petrified scum, half-empty soft-drink cans, apple cores, remnants of an ant farm—the inhabitants of which have mysteriously disappeared—a gerbil cage with two forlorn gerbils miraculously still alive within it.

Messy Room

Mindi likes her room this way. Her friends like her room this way. Her mother gets a sick headache every time she sees it.

RESOLUTION:

1. Don't feed into the problem—in other words, no nagging.
2. State your expectation: "By Saturday morning, I expect everything to be in order."
3. Tell your child that there will be no Saturday activities until the room passes inspection.
4. Use the "When . . . then" positive incentive: "When your room is clean, then you can have a friend stay overnight."
5. Sit down with your child and plan ahead. You might say, "One of my jobs as a parent is to help you develop habits of neatness." Involve your child in setting up rewards and encouragements for keeping a clean room, as well as consequences for a messy room. You might want to help develop guidelines for what a clean room is.

A "clean room" has its:

- ☑ bed made
- ☑ floor picked up
- ☑ clean clothes put away
- ☑ drawers pushed in
- ☑ dirty clothes sent down

Note: If the bedroom is extremely messy, as is the case with Mindi, you might want to help your child organize the room. This provides the child with extra attention and allows you to teach her how to get things done.

If your child is over ten and there are other major concerns such as drugs or concern about sexual activities, you may want to save your energy for them and just close the door and do a once-a-month health check for creepy-crawly things.

Undesirable Friends

Andrea comes home from her first day in high school with a new friend. The friend's hair matches the colors in the floral bouquet on the table. She is wearing so many earrings in her left ear that the weight of the metal causes her head to tip markedly to one side.

"This is B.J.," says Andrea to her mom.

"How do you do, B.J." Mom answers in her most calculatedly cheerful voice. "Would you like to hang up your studded-leather jacket in the closet?"

"Naw, I'll keep it on. Covers up the bruises," B.J. answers.

"Bruises? How did you get bruises?" asks Mom, afraid of what she is going to hear.

"From my old man," B.J. says, fishing in her pocket for a cigarette.

"Your father hits you?" Andrea's mother asks with genuine horror.

Undesirable Friends

"Naw, not my father—you know, my boyfriend. We were just foolin' around."

"He rides the coolest motorcycle, Mom," Andrea says excitedly. "He told me he'd take me for a ride tomorrow after school. Isn't that great?"

Mom sees her life flash before her eyes.

Congratulations to this mom. In spite of her misgivings, she is keeping the line of communication open with her daughter and her daughter's new friend.

RESOLUTION:

1. Express your concerns to your child: "I'm concerned about your safety on a motorcycle."
2. Set limits—for instance, your child can see her new friend, but only at your house. Empathize with her feelings but insist that there be no motorcycle riding. ("It's my job as a parent to watch out for your safety and well-being. . . .")
3. Spend time with the new friend so you can more accurately assess possible risks.
4. In extreme cases, no contact at all can be allowed with the undesirable friend. Be clear and direct with both your child and her friend. Tell them exactly why you disapprove of the friend's behavior. For instance, if the friend's dishonesty is apparent, you might say, "Lying and stealing are not allowed in our home. You are not welcome here because I don't want you to influence my child." Be firm and calm.

HOW TO SOLVE COMMON PROBLEMS

FIVE KEYS TO SUCCESS

- Don't respond to uproar
- Restate your expectations or concerns
- Offer "When . . . then" incentives
- Use the magic word . . . "nevertheless"
- Think ahead: plan together for a mutually "happy" resolution

HOW TO SOLVE COMMON PROBLEMS

FIVE KEYS TO SUCCESS...

✓ DON'T RESPOND TO UPROAR

✓ RESTATE YOUR EXPECTATIONS OR CONCERNS

✓ OFFER THE "WHEN...THEN" INCENTIVE

✓ USE THE MAGIC WORD "NEVERTHELESS"

✓ THINK AHEAD: PLAN TOGETHER FOR A MUTUALLY "HAPPY" RESOLUTION

Dispense ad lib _____ *Carolyn Ann Meeks* _____ M.D.

4 • Great Expectations

Do not attempt to teach a pig to sing. It's a waste of your time and annoying to the pig.
—Farmer's Almanac

There are a lot of frustrated parents who, because of unrealistic expectations, have been attempting to teach the proverbial pig to sing. Parents who expect their newborn to sleep peacefully through the night and not to cry when he's awake. Parents who expect their two-year-old not to fuss and squirm and crawl under the table in a restaurant. Parents who expect their teenager not to rebel.

Sometimes the only thing it takes for these well-meaning moms and dads to relax and start enjoying their children is to realize what's normal behavior for a particular age group.

TERRIFIC TODDLERS SAY "NO"

Two months before Mikie's second birthday, the normally complacent, altogether delightful little moppet began displaying a stubborn, self-willed streak that had his parents concerned. By the time they made an appointment to see me several months later, they were at their wits' end.

"He says 'no' to everything," Mikie's mom said. "Even things he likes and wants he says 'no' to!"

"He's turning into a real monster!" Dad chimed in.

I looked over at the little towhead, playing contentedly with colored blocks and a toy car. He caught my glance and smiled, then went back to his block-building pursuits.

I asked the parents if they realized it's normal for all two-year-olds to begin asserting their independence by saying no—that not only is it normal, in fact, but it is an important part of their development. I suggested that perhaps they were concerned because they had unrealistic expectations of just what a two-year-old is like, when instead they could be pleased that Mikie was right on track in his behavior.

"Well, maybe it's normal, but it's still making us nuts," Dad said. "Isn't there something we can do to get us through this time?" And indeed there is.

1. Offer choices.

Whenever possible, give your two-year-old a choice. If naptime is becoming a hassle, ask him if he wants a story before he takes his nap or when he wakes up. Instead of telling him to wash his hands for dinner, you can ask him if he wants to wash his hands by himself or if he would like you

Terrific Toddlers (Say "No")

to help him. (If your child does not want to wash his hands himself, let him know you will need to help him.)

2. Allow situations where your child can say "no" and congratulate him on his ability to think for himself.

Remember, your role is to guide, not to control. So let there be times when you allow your child to assert his preference without considering it a threat to your role as a parent. For example, you might say, "Would you like to wear your blue suspenders with those pants?" or "Would you like to come with me while I water the lawn?" Let your child know that you notice he has found a new way to do things or has an opinion about something. It will give him a healthy sense of self, and will actually help him when he becomes a teenager to say no to peer pressure.

3. Put yourself in your child's place.

Imagine a world where everybody is three times bigger than you—a world filled with a whole array of fascinating things to crawl over, crawl under, explore, and put in your mouth. Public places like restaurants and grocery stores can be very difficult because you're not allowed to use your high energy; some playful distraction will help you to pass the time in these situations (see below). If you learn to see things from his perspective it can be a wonderful learning experience for you both.

4. Try to distract your child.

You can avoid many unnecessary conflicts with your toddler by redirecting his attention past the things that he is likely to say "no" to. You might for instance:

- Offer to tell him a story (you make it up) about a child with the same name as his and an animal like "Toby the cat."
- Make a game out of finding the items you need at the grocery store.
- Play a game with the napkins while you're waiting in a restaurant. Keep small gadgets and toys on hand that you can pull out only on such occasions.
- Try singing "Twinkle, Twinkle, Little Star" together (even if you don't think you can sing).

You are more creative than you think. Toddlers know when they have your attention, and they tend to be easily distracted from saying "no" unnecessarily.

5. Set limits.

Limits allow your child to feel protected. All children need them and want them. Without them, they become anxious and insecure. It's up to you to set the limits, and up to you to enforce them. So, when it comes down to the well-being of you and your child, you need to follow through, no matter how much he might protest.

QUESTIONING PRESCHOOLERS

If you've ever taken an afternoon drive with a four-year-old, you know what it's like: "Are we there yet?" "How long till we get there?" "What's that sign say?" "How come cows have those things hanging down?" "How much longer?"

Four-year-olds can easily drive you crazy with their questions. They are starting to explore their world. Everything is interesting and new and exciting. They want all of your time all of the time to explain everything to them and enjoy it with them.

In many parts of the world, extended families are the rule rather than the exception, and that's really what a four-year-old needs. No one adult can satisfy *all* the needs of this inquisitive age group. And no one parent has the patience to answer every single question.

A four-year-old needs to have multiple resources, and his parents need to have a reprieve from what can be a mind-numbing barrage of questions and demands for attention.

Here are some tips to help you deal with the Questioning Fours:

1. Create an Extended family.

Adopt a grandma if you don't have one who lives nearby. Enlist the aid of neighbors and friends. Bring in relatives. There are lots of people who would love to share the energy and enthusiasm of your four-year-old!

Questioning Preschoolers

2. Accept your limitations.

Realize you're only one person with a lot of demands on your time and your energy. There is only so much you can do to satisfy the insatiable needs of a pesky four-year-old. Be willing to be happily imperfect.

3. Import playmates.

If your child goes to preschool or kindergarten, invite a classmate over for an hour or two, or arrange to have your child visit at a friend's house a few times a week.

4. Hire an eight-year-old.

An eight-year-old makes a perfect companion for your preschooler. For twenty-five cents an hour, you can hire a neighbor child to play with your four-year-old and they'll both be delighted. You'll need to be there to supervise, of course, but the two of them will find plenty to do without needing to involve you.

5. Set aside special time for exploring questions.

You may not be able to give your child the quantity of time he would like, but you can make sure that the time you do spend with him is his alone. The next time he asks you where the stars go during the day, you can say, "That's an important question. Let's write it down so we don't forget, and when we have our special time together we'll talk about it."

DEBATING GRADE SCHOOLERS

"Come home right after school," Tina's mom tells her eight-year-old as the child gathers up her lunch, her milk money, and a jar of pollywogs for her science project.

"How come I always have to come home right after school?" Tina demands, plopping the pollywogs back on the kitchen counter. "Everybody else gets to stay and play on the playground. What's the difference if I play here or there? How come you get to make all the rules, anyway?"

Life with a third-grader can be a challenge for parents who don't realize that it's normal for eight-year-olds to argue about everything.

At this age, children are developing their intellectual reasoning skills, and they use their parents as sounding boards. You can expect them to disagree about the limits you've set and to disagree with the idea that you're the one who gets to set the limits in the first place. And often, you can expect them to be very convincing in their arguments.

It's important to remember when interacting with your child that it's O.K. to yield from time to time. Just because you give in when their argument is sound doesn't mean you've lost control as a parent.

Here are some ways to deal positively with your debating eight-year-old:

1. Let your child know it's O.K. to disagree.

It is important for your child to feel comfortable expressing her opinions and discussing her feelings openly with you. However, it is equally important for her to know a discussion doesn't have to mean an argument. Help your child discern the difference. If your child never debates or disagrees, she may need you to encourage her actively to develop preferences. You will want her to be able to know what she feels, to be able to formulate opinions and to stand up for herself. The best place to practice is at home.

2. Listen to what your child has to say.

Active listening is very important with all age groups, but it's particularly important that you let your eight-year-old know you've heard what she said. Feed her comments back to her: "What I hear you saying is that you'd like to stay and play after school with your friends."

3. Look for the truth in what she says.

Try to find a grain of truth or some point of agreement in what your child has to say and acknowledge it, even if it just means acknowledging her feelings: "Well, if I were you, I guess I'd like to stay and play after school, too."

4. Present your point of view.

Tell your child what you see as the problem and what you see as the options for its solution: "I understand that you want to stay at school and play with your friends, but as far as I know there's no adult there to supervise. I don't know why your friends are allowed to stay there, but I do know I care about you."

Debating Grade Schoolers

5. Lighten up!

Grade-school age can be one of the most fun and exciting age ranges of all. Enjoy your child in this special time of her life. Relax. Work through the issues but try to keep some perspective. You are on the same team with your child.

TENACIOUS TEENS

When fifteen-year-old Matt's dad gave him money for a haircut and his son came home with the left side of his head shaved clean and the right side still down around his eyebrows, Dad freaked. "What are you planning to do, join a side show?" he yelled.

Matt just shrugged. "I like it this way. It's my hair; I ought to be able to wear it any way I want."

"Not while you live in THIS house," Dad said, quickly realizing there was not a single thing he could to do about it at that point.

Whether it's a bizarre haircut, sneaking out at night, not doing homework, using the family car without permission, or any of a hundred others things your teenager might do to create a crisis, it's important to realize that each act is done not so much out of rebellion, but in an attempt to separate from the parents.

It is not uncommon for a teenager:

• To say, "I hate you."

Tenacious Teens

- To blame, "You're unfair!"
- To say, "You're mean."
- To accuse, "You never listen to me!"
- To be embarrassed by you because you're not "cool."
- To think that you are somehow inadequate as a parent.

The irony of the situation is that the more bonding there is in the early years between parent and child, the more outrageous the child's behavior is apt to be when it comes time for the break. Although it is distressing, all of this is to be expected.

Think about it this way: If your teenager didn't turn just slightly weird, you'd probably want him to hang around forever. And if there weren't some conflict between the two of you, he might agree to do that. So, for both your sakes, the separation needs to take place. If you had a warm, supportive relationship in the early years, chances are excellent that you will once again. By the time he's thirty or so, he will usually snap back to the value system you instilled in him when he was young.

But before you throw up your hands in despair over the inevitability of separation trauma, there are some very effective things you can do to circumvent or minimize the need for your teen to create crises.

1. Don't take your teenager's behavior personally.

If what he says is "I hate you!" realize that it's normal. One very wise parent told her fourteen-year-old, "I hear what you're saying, but I won't hold you to it." Recognize what all the uproar is about—which is usually not the issues at hand, but the need for him to find some way of enraging you so you'll want him to be on his own. Just make sure your teen knows that while you may dislike the behavior, you still love the person. "I love you. I just don't like your haircut. But I will try to learn to live with it." Respect your child's need to become independent, no matter what craziness he may be acting out in the moment. If he is acting very distant, let him know that it's O.K., and let him know that he can always come back.

2. Be an active listener.

Listen to the words your teen says and the words he doesn't say. Identify his feelings as well as the content and feed it back to him: "You're angry." "I understand what you're feeling; you feel I'm unfair."

3. Let your child know it's your job to set reasonable limits.

"It's my job as a parent to help you learn to be responsible and to provide a setting where you can best learn it. I wouldn't be a good parent if I let you get away with using the car without permission, and that's why I'm going to take away all car privileges for two weeks." Be sure you explain why you're about to revoke privileges. Assume that your teen is smart—he'll understand the logic.

4. Share your own history with your teen.

Teenagers don't want you to tell them what to do, but they do want to know what your experiences were and how you handled them when you were an adolescent. Stay away from preaching to your child. Rather, share your humanness with him. Tell him how you felt when you were a teenager, how you dealt with all the uncertainties of adolescence. Talk about your experiences with things like peer pressure, school cliques, homework, social attitudes, and sexuality. Tell him about the decisions you made at his age, both the good ones and the ones you later regretted. Both you and your teen are likely to benefit from this kind of exchange.

5. Let your teenager know that it's O.K. to have some secrets.

It is normal and healthy for your teenager to have some private thoughts that he won't share with you. This is part of the differentiation process of making the transition from teenager to adulthood. During this period in his life, time spent with his peers is extremely important. Your adolescent may also form a close friendship with another adult such as a teacher, counselor, or a friend's parent. It is very important for you to realize that all of this is perfectly normal and is to be encouraged.

6. Be a good role model.

Your primary responsibility to your teenager is to be a good role model for how to treat other people, how to work out disagreements, how to be happy in your life.

TIPS TO DEAL WITH TODDLERS

(EXPECT YOUR TODDLER TO SAY "NO")

- Offer choices
- Congratulate him on his ability to think for himself
- Put yourself in your child's place
- Try to distract your child
- Set limits

CAROLYN ANN MEEKS M.D. ● Prescriptions for Parenting

R TIPS TO DEAL WITH TODDLERS

(EXPECT YOUR TODDLER TO SAY "NO")

- ✓ OFFER CHOICES
- ✓ CONGRATULATE YOUR CHILD ON HIS ABILITY TO THINK FOR HIMSELF
- ✓ PUT YOURSELF IN YOUR CHILD'S PLACE
- ✓ TRY TO DISTRACT YOUR CHILD
- ✓ SET LIMITS

 Dispense ad lib _____ Carolyn Ann Meeks _____ M.D.

TIPS TO DEAL WITH PRESCHOOLERS

(EXPECT YOUR PRESCHOOLERS TO DRIVE YOU CRAZY WITH QUESTIONS)

- Create an extended family
- Accept your limitations
- Import playmates
- Hire an eight-year-old
- Set aside special time for exploring questions

TIPS TO DEAL WITH PRESCHOOLERS

(EXPECT YOUR PRESCHOOLERS TO DRIVE YOU CRAZY WITH QUESTIONS)

✓ CREATE AN EXTENDED FAMILY

✓ ACCEPT YOUR LIMITATIONS

✓ IMPORT PLAYMATES

✓ HIRE AN EIGHT-YEAR-OLD

✓ SET ASIDE SPECIAL TIME FOR EXPLORING QUESTIONS

Dispense ad lib _____ *Carolyn Ann Meeks* _____ M.D.

TIPS TO DEAL WITH GRADE SCHOOLERS

(EXPECT YOUR GRADE SCHOOLER TO DEBATE WITH YOU ABOUT EVERYTHING)

- Let your child know it's O.K. to disagree
- Listen to what your child has to say
- Look for the truth in what he says
- Present your point of view
- Lighten up!

 TIPS TO DEAL WITH GRADE SCHOOLERS

(EXPECT YOUR GRADE SCHOOLER TO DEBATE WITH YOU ABOUT EVERYTHING)

- ✓ LET YOUR CHILD KNOW IT'S O.K. TO DISAGREE
- ✓ LISTEN TO WHAT YOUR CHILD HAS TO SAY
- ✓ LOOK FOR THE TRUTH IN WHAT HE SAYS
- ✓ PRESENT YOUR POINT OF VIEW
- ✓ LIGHTEN UP!

 Dispense ad lib _____ Carolyn Ann Meeks _____ M.D.

TIPS TO DEAL WITH TEENS

(EXPECT SOME "OUTRAGEOUS" BEHAVIOR)

- Don't take your teenager's behavior personally

- Be an active listener

- Let your child know it's your job to set reasonable limits

- Share your own history with your teen

- Let your teenager know it's O.K. to have some secrets

- Be a good role model

 TIPS TO DEAL WITH TEENS
(EXPECT SOME "OUTRAGEOUS" BEHAVIOR)

✓ DON'T TAKE YOUR TEENAGER'S BEHAVIOR PERSONALLY

✓ BE AN ACTIVE LISTENER

✓ LET YOUR CHILD KNOW IT'S YOUR JOB TO SET REASONABLE LIMITS

✓ SHARE YOUR OWN HISTORY WITH YOUR TEEN

✓ LET YOUR TEENAGER KNOW IT'S O.K. TO HAVE SOME SECRETS

✓ BE A GOOD ROLE MODEL

 Dispense ad lib _____ *Carolyn Ann Meeks* _____ M.D.

Part II • ENRICHED PARENTING

5 • Five Ways to Avoid Power Struggles

1. Remember, most misbehavior is an appeal for love. (Don't take it personally.)

"I HATE YOU! You don't care about me!" eight-year-old Lisa cried. "If you REALLY loved me you would let me spend the night at Becky's. You probably had me just to have somebody to be mean to. You probably wouldn't even care if I ran away!"

It may be hard to picture Lisa's foot-stomping, door-slamming snit as an appeal for love, but that's exactly what it is. In fact, many acts of misbehavior are nothing more than just that.

The grouchy child, the child throwing a tantrum, the child who tells you she hates you—all of these behaviors reflect a child who is not feeling very good about herself. Instead of thinking that your child is attacking you personally, try to remember that your child actually needs love at this time. Your child may need you to give love by setting limits or by empowering her to help you solve the problem. Doing this reassures her that you love her, even if you don't like her behavior.

This mother might say, "Lisa, I don't like your behavior right now. I *do* love you. Take a time-out to think about what I've said. When you're ready to behave in a way that you can be proud of, we'll sit down and talk about it."

So the next time your child acts up or acts out, if you can remember that her misbehavior may simply be an appeal for love, it will be easier for you to give her what she needs while not getting caught up in the drama she's creating.

2. Remind your child you're on the same team.

The next time your child flies into a tantrum over some perceived injustice on your part, instead of confronting him, becoming defensive, or just plain getting mad, simply put your arm around his shoulder and say, "I know it may not seem to be true right now, but we're on the same team." Put yourself at eye level and be sure to make eye contact.

A friend of mine tried this with her eight-year-old son, John, who wanted to play ball in the busy street in front of their house. He was angry and frustrated when his mother wouldn't let him. After giving John a few minutes to cool off, she went over to him, put her arm around him, told him how much she loved him, and reminded him that they were really on the same team. She could almost feel the gentle melting away of his resistance.

It worked equally well for the mother of a teenager who faced the wrath of her daughter when the skating rink was put off-limits because of a problem with drugs on the premises.

Remember, most misbehavior is an appeal for love. (Don't take it personally.)

"Everybody else gets to go," fourteen-year-old Terri wailed. "Jenny's mom lets HER go every single week!"

Terri's mom put her arm on her daughter's shoulder and said, "I don't know about Jenny's situation, but I do know I care about you. I understand how upset you are about this. We're on the same team."

3. Don't expect perfection from yourself or from your child.

How many times have you heard someone say, "That kid really knows how to push my button!"? Often, children seem to exit the womb knowing exactly how to create maximum disruption—and precisely when to do it.

It's Thursday evening. Your day has been a killer. Your boss yelled at you. Your customers yelled at you. The baby-sitter called to say she thinks she's coming down with chicken pox. You just found out it's going to cost $450 to fix the car that was supposedly fixed last week. You are exhausted, feeling sorry for yourself, and on the verge of tears.

Before you have even put the car in the garage, an idea is percolating in the mind of your offspring: "BUTTON, BUTTON, LET'S PUSH THE BUTTON!"

You walk in the door and POW!

Nine-year-old Suzie says she's never going back to school EVER. Her teacher's mean and all the kids hate her and make fun of her. She got eleven wrong on her spelling test because you didn't help her study for it last night. And the school nurse tested her eyes and she can't see ANYTHING. . . .

You, who are already feeling put-upon, unfairly treated, and tired to the bone, are suddenly

Remind your child you're on the same team.

Don't expect perfection from yourself or from your child.

overwhelmed with a feeling that you have failed as a mother! Your daughter got a D on her spelling test, she's got bad eyes, nobody likes her . . . and it's all your fault!

You do what many normal mothers would do under the circumstances. You yell at Suzie for never studying, tell her her eyes are bad because she watches too much television, then you go into your room, close the door, and cry. Operation Button-Push has been a resounding success.

If, on the other hand, you had realized your vulnerability on the way home, understood that you were probably going to be more sensitive to the carryings-on of your children, you might have said to Suzie, "Boy, we both had a bad day, didn't we? Come here and give me a hug—I bet that will help."

Becoming aware of your sensitive areas and developing realistic expectations of yourself and your children can be helpful in avoiding power struggles and maintaining control of your buttons.

4. Deal with conflict, don't hide from it.

Unless you're living alone on top of a mountain (in which case you probably wouldn't be reading this book) or have somehow given birth to a family of robots, there's a pretty good chance you're going to have to face the issue of conflict in your life. Conflict implies disagreement, which is normal, healthy, and inevitable. It doesn't have to entail fighting.

Different people have different ideas, opinions, and preferences. There's nothing wrong with that. Mom likes red; Jessica prefers blue. Adam likes Mexican food; Mary likes Chinese.

It's only when we believe our ideas, opinions, and preferences are "right" and everyone else's are "wrong"—or are afraid to voice a dissenting opinion—that we get into trouble. The first position

119

Deal with conflict; don't hide from it.

leads to a form of autocratic rule that is sure to be challenged. The second can lead to repressed anger, depression, and even ill health.

If Adam convinced the family to go out for Mexican food because he liked it, even though he knew it made his sister sick to her stomach and burned his brother's mouth so badly he couldn't brush his teeth for two days, he could expect a healthy challenge on his hands. If, however, in an attempt to be compliant, "nice" children, Mary and Randy ended up in Rosa's Cantina without voicing their opinion and needs, they would probably grumble, argue, fidget, and be generally unpleasant throughout the meal, and add another unexpressed grievance to what was probably a growing list.

Children need to know it's O.K. to disagree. Learning to talk about their opinions and feelings is a sign of healthy development in children and should be encouraged.

Parents who hide their feelings and don't resolve problems as they arise will find that these unresolved problems collect, which may end up weakening a relationship—or their health—and teaching their children, by example, to do the same.

It's important to teach children to confront and resolve conflict rather than save up problems in the interest of being "nice."

5. Take good care of yourself.

One of the best ways to avoid power struggles is to take good care of yourself. If you're relaxed, happy, and full of energy, you'll be a lot better able to sidestep the "yes-you-will-no-I-won't" syndrome when little Stephanie flies into a tantrum over something you've asked her to do.

If, on the other hand, you're tired, mopey, and tense, the tiniest incident can quickly escalate into World War III.

HOW TO PREVENT A CRISIS

• *Exercise.* An hour three times a week or thirty minutes five times a week of jogging, swimming, biking, or brisk walking will go a long way toward keeping you resilient—physically and emotionally.

• *Meditate, relax, or daydream.* Allow time in your day to just *be*—to relax and renew your spirit as well as your body, to find that place of inner peace that's there just waiting for you.

• *Touch.* Touch is therapeutic. Even something as simple as a handshake, holding your child, giving (and receiving) a hug. Back rubs, neck rubs, and massages can change a mood fast.

• *Mini-vacations.* Can't get away for the weekend? How about for an hour? And you don't even have to leave home. Just get out the bubble bath, light some scented candles, put on your favorite music and . . . Bliss City! Or hire a baby-sitter, enlist a friend, or ask a relative to watch Timmy and Tony while you go to a movie or have a quiet dinner out.

Getting away for frequent short periods is actually more beneficial than infrequent longer breaks.

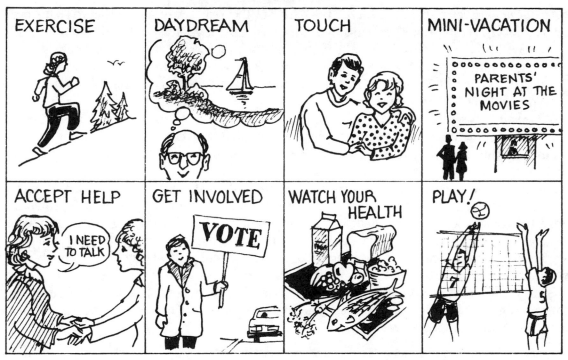

Take good care of yourself.

• *Accept help.* Ever notice that there's no Martyr-of-the-Year award for mothers? That's probably because martyrs create more problems than they cure for themselves and their kids. So resist the urge to say, "No, that's O.K.," when a friend, relative, or spouse offers help. Look into getting counseling or join a support group if you're having trouble coping. In fact, if you want help and it isn't offered, ask for it! There's no rule that says you have to be everything to everybody. What's more, you couldn't be, even if you tried.

• *Get involved.* An interesting person is an interested person. Find something you *love*, something you *believe in*, something you *care about*, and get involved. It will keep you feeling young, interesting, and alive. It will make your kids more fun to come home to, and it will make you more fun to be with.

• *Pay attention to your physical health.* Junk the junk food, even if it is quick and easy. Take the time to provide balanced meals, not only for your child, but for yourself as well. You'll see the change this can make in your mood. Just as important as what you eat is getting enough rest. If there don't seem to be enough hours in the day for you to take a break, be creative with your rest time. Lie down on the carpet while your children are playing. Snuggle up on the couch and have your child tell you a story!

• *Play.* We all need play in our lives. Not two-year-old play or ten-year-old play. Grown-up play. Whatever is *fun for us*. Figure out what makes you happy—what makes your heart sing—and do it for at least a few minutes every day!

Life can be a wondrous experience if you give yourself permission to take care of *you*. At the same time, you'll be giving your children one of the greatest gifts of all—a role model for how to be responsible for your own joyful well-being.

FIVE WAYS TO AVOID POWER STRUGGLES

- Remember, most misbehavior is an appeal for love . . . don't take it personally
- Remind your child you're on the same team
- Don't expect perfection from yourself or your child
- Deal with conflict; don't hide from it
- Take good care of yourself

 FIVE WAYS TO AVOID POWER STRUGGLES

✓ REMEMBER, MOST MISBEHAVIOR IS AN APPEAL FOR LOVE...DON'T TAKE IT PERSONALLY

✓ REMIND YOUR CHILD YOU'RE ON THE SAME TEAM

✓ DON'T EXPECT PERFECTION FROM YOURSELF OR YOUR CHILD

✓ DEAL WITH CONFLICT; DON'T HIDE FROM IT

✓ TAKE GOOD CARE OF YOURSELF

 Dispense ad lib _____ *Carolyn Ann Meeks* _____ M.D.

6 • Five Ways to Unhook from a Power Struggle

I t's happened. In spite of all your good intentions, you and Ivan the Terrible are heavy at it, embroiled in an argument. No time for avoidance techniques—you need help *now*.

The first thing to do is try to gain some perspective on why Ivan is in such a snit. All you said was, "No, you can't have what you want right now."

1. Try to see the situation from your child's perspective.

For just a minute, imagine what it would be like if a couple of giants came to live at your house—they told you what to wear, what to eat, when to go to bed, when to get up, what you could (and couldn't) watch on TV, and when you had to take a bath.

Try to see the situation from your child's perspective.

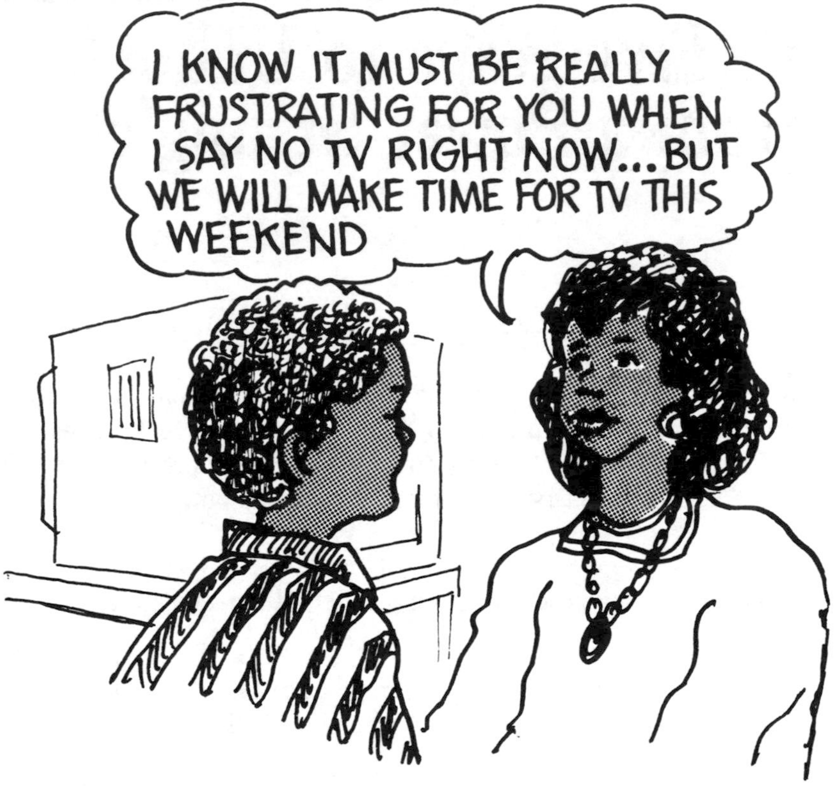

No matter how well-meaning and benevolent the giants might be, chances are, the whole scene would soon become irksome. Try to see any conflict from your child's perspective. Empathizing with your child is often helpful because it allows you to step back, effectively ending the power struggle before it has a chance to go any further. "I know it must be really frustrating for you when I say no TV right now, but we will make more time for that this weekend."

2. Use the "feel-felt-found" technique.

Here is a sequential technique that has met with *great* success. Try it.

THE "FEEL-FELT-FOUND" TECHNIQUE

Feel

- Identify your child's feeling—e.g., angry, frustrated, upset.
- Say, "It looks to me like you're *feeling* really angry."

This gives an opportunity for your child to verify his exact feeling. He might say, "Yeah, I'm really mad." If he says, "No, I'm frustrated," restate his feeling: "So you're really frustrated right now." You have now validated his feeling.

Use the "feel-felt-found" technique.

Felt

- Next try to find some small grain of truth in your child's argument or battle with you. For example, try to think of some time that you've felt frustrated.
- Say, "I know how you feel. I've *felt* that way, too. When I was a teenager, my dad used to turn off the TV right in the middle of a program."

Found

- Now share some resolution or tip that you have found helpful in your life.
- Say, "What I *found* was that if I did my chores and homework, it was much easier to negotiate for extra TV time."

This sequence often works like magic. Your child knows you understand—realizes you've been through the same thing and found a way to resolve it. The technique works especially well with teens whose number one complaint is that no one understands them. They want to know your experiences so they can better decide for themselves how to handle similar situations in their own lives. This is a nonintrusive way of sharing experiences as you begin allowing your older child to resolve his own problems.

3. Have your child take a time-out.

You've empathized yourself into a stupor. You've tried twenty versions of "feel-felt-found," and Hilary is still hysterical. You have a full-fledged tantrum on your hands. There's no point trying to carry on any kind of meaningful communication until she has had a chance to calm down and both she and you have had an opportunity to gain some perspective on the situation. It's time for a time-out.

Time-out can be used as an opportunity to cool off. Assume that your child wants to behave in a way that she can be proud of. A cooling-off period is valuable for that purpose.

Important: If your child is old enough to reason, ask her to think about possible solutions to the issue at hand during the time-out.

Idea:

A large open box—about the size a television set comes in—labeled "Fuss Box" is a great idea* for children from eighteen months to three years. When a toddler is having a tantrum, you can say that it's fine if she wants to fuss, but it will have to be done in the Fuss Box. If she is ready to stop the tantrum, she can come out. If not, you can say, "I see you're not ready to stop. When you are, you can come out."

---

*Adapted from *WE Newsletter* (1982) by Jean Clarke, author of *Self-Esteem: A Family Affair*.

Have your child take a time-out.

4. In case of rage, *you* take a time-out.

If you're feeling excessively enraged, give yourself a chance to cool off and think about what's happening. Some psychologists call this a "reverse time-out."

Put your child some place safe where he can't hurt himself. Then simply remove yourself from your child and go to the bathroom, bedroom, or any place else where you can relax and think things over. Sit down, call a friend or the nearest crisis clinic—do whatever it takes to regain your composure.

I find it very helpful to write down a few notes describing the incident at hand.

Then try to figure out why this situation made you so angry. For example:

- ☐ I felt powerless.
- ☐ I felt I should have had better control over my child.
- ☐ I felt hurt, so I overreacted.
- ☐ I had a bad day (week, year), and I was taking my stress out on my kid.
- ☐ Other _____

Formulate a possible plan. For example:

- ☐ Wait till we are both cooled off.
- ☐ Apologize for "losing it."
- ☐ Remind my child: "We're on the same team."
- ☐ Involve him in the resolution of the problem. Say, "How can we make this a better situation for both of us?"

In case of rage, *you* take a time-out.

Sometimes parents feel a sense of duty to follow through as soon as there is any misbehavior. Just remember, no great psychological damage is going to occur—to your child or to you—if you don't handle every situation as it comes up. If you're feeling out of control, give yourself the time you need. Remember it's O.K. if you lose a few points occasionally, as long as you and your child win the game.

5. Ask yourself what's more important to you—the love of power or the power of love?

Power struggles happen when a parent wants to control a child and his behavior, rather than help the child develop an internal set of values and standards and his own sense of responsibility. If you become dictatorial every time your child disagrees with you, he will receive the message that it's not O.K. for him to have his own thoughts, his own ideas, his own wishes, his own preferences—or his own feelings. He may eventually become compliant, and a few years down the road you may find yourself saying to him, "Just because your friends are doing it doesn't mean you have to! Don't you have a mind of your own?" Realize that your job is to guide, not to control.

Ask yourself what's more important to you—the love of power or the power of love?

FIVE WAYS TO UNHOOK FROM A POWER STRUGGLE

- Try to see the situation from your child's perspective
- Use the "feel-felt-found" technique
- Have your child take a time-out
- In case of rage . . . YOU take a time-out
- Ask yourself what's more important to you . . . the love of power or the power of love

 FIVE WAYS TO UNHOOK FROM A POWER STRUGGLE

✓ TRY TO SEE THE SITUATION FROM YOUR CHILD'S PERSPECTIVE

✓ USE THE "FEEL-FELT-FOUND" TECHNIQUE

✓ HAVE YOUR CHILD TAKE A TIME-OUT

✓ IN CASE OF RAGE... **YOU** TAKE A TIME-OUT

✓ ASK YOURSELF WHAT'S MORE IMPORTANT TO YOU...THE LOVE OF POWER OR THE POWER OF LOVE

 Dispense ad lib _____ Carolyn Ann Meeks _____ M.D.

7 • Five Steps to Help Your Child Become Independent and Responsible

If you have learned to avoid or unhook from a power struggle, congratulations! Now you are ready to go on to the constructive resolution of the problem. The following five steps will help your child to become responsible. They are applicable for any of a myriad of typical behavioral problems—from sibling rivalry to procrastination of chores or of homework. These steps are:

1. Actively listen to your child.

The first step to resolving any problem with your child is allowing him to explain his feelings and letting him know you have listened to him. Listening to his opinions, preferences, and emotions is one of the most important things you can do. Let your child sound off. He may complain about

Actively listen to your child.

unfairness, give excuses for inexcusable behavior, or tell you a rambling, pointless story that is so long you're sure you're going to be ready for a rest-home before he's done. But stay with it. Listen attentively and respond with empathy. It will help your child diffuse his emotions, and it will help you understand your child.

When a panel of teenagers met recently at a student leaders' conference, they all agreed that if they could say just one thing to parents with children of all ages, it would be to really listen to them—give them feedback to show that they had heard and understood; empathize with their dilemmas.

Suppose you have just given ten-year-old Jason a time-out for trying to throw his older sister's makeup in the wastebasket. "The thing that bugs me is that just because she's a GIRL, she thinks she owns the bathroom," Jason says about his sister. "She uses all the hot water and leaves disgusting GIRL things all over and gets MAKEUP on all the towels, and I'm always late for everything because I can never get in there!"

Listen to whatever your child wants to say, and help him identify his feelings. Here are a few possible responses that might help Jason feel better:

"You seem to be really upset."
"You feel like Jill isn't being very considerate of your needs."
"That must really bother you."

Usually, your child will respond with a sense of relief that finally somebody understands how he feels.

2. Tell your child out loud that you care.

Children know what their role is—to play, to eat, to get their way, to outgrow their clothes every two weeks, to make as much noise as possible, to need braces, and periodically to make you crazy.

What they need a reminder of is *your* role as parent and guardian of their health, welfare, and safety—and of your commitment to that role. Tell your child out loud that you care.

When your child does something that could cause harm to himself or others or worry to you, he needs to be made accountable for his actions.

When nine-year-old Kate is two hours late getting home from school and then can't understand what all the fuss is about, you say, "It's my job as a parent to know where you are, and when you don't call I get concerned that something may have happened to you."

Even very young children will understand your need for their accountability. And most will respond admirably—especially if the next time Kate calls from her friend's house, you acknowledge it and notice the improvement, or just thank her.

3. Admit to your child that you can't solve the problem alone.

Before three to five years of age, children need help developing structure and setting limits. After five, they need to begin participating in the process. Take eleven-year-old Andrew, for example. It isn't that he hates doing the dishes—or even that it takes him very long to do them. It's just that he has so many other things he'd rather be doing. Night after night he procrastinates.

Tell your child out loud that you care.

"Andrew, have you done the dishes?"

"Not yet, Mom, but I will."

"When, Andrew?"

"Just as soon as I finish what I'm doing."

An hour later:

"Andrew, are you doing the dishes?"

"Not yet, Mom, but I will in five minutes."

Five minutes later:

"O.K., Andrew, the five minutes are up. Do the dishes."

"I'm doing something REALLY important, Mom, and I'm almost finished. I promise I'll do the dishes as soon as I'm done."

Half an hour later:

"Are the dishes done, Andrew?"

"It's late, Mom, and I'm really tired. Can I do them in the morning?"

"DO THE DISHES NOW, OR YOU WON'T LIVE TO SEE MORNING!"

Even though Andrew doesn't see this evasion ritual as a particular problem, his mom does. And something needs to be done.

Tell your child that you need his input to resolve the problem. Mom might say, "Son, I need your help. Every night we go through this business with the dishes. Frankly, I can't solve the problem alone." Appealing to him in this way gives him a sense of ownership of the resolution to the problem. Now you're ready for the next step.

4. Empower your child to solve the problem.

With a toddler who is misbehaving, you will want to create encouragements and provide consequences. With children three to five years of age, you can begin to involve your child in resolving problems. Ask your child to think of or make a list of possible resolutions for any given problem. If he doesn't come up with an idea right away, give him more time to think. (Postponing playtime for a younger child or TV and phone time for an older child speeds up the process considerably.) This may anger your child, but if you *don't* take this step, *you* may be the one who is angry; ignore his uproar and proceed.

Encourage him to offer solutions, even if he thinks they're not great ones. At that point, you're liable to get answers like, "Well, we could eat off paper plates and then there wouldn't be any dishes to wash"; or "You could do the dishes for me." But hang in there.

If your child can't think of one single solution, you can offer an example or two to get him started. But save this as a last resort.

Writing out your child's ideas can be very helpful in showing him you believe they're valuable.

Later, when there are several options on the table, you can ask him which one he considers the most useful.

"O.K., let's say you wait until morning to do the dishes. How much longer do you think it will take you to do them after the food is caked on as hard as cement? How much earlier are you going to have to get up in order to do them? How much earlier are you going to have to go to bed at night to still get enough sleep?"

Look at the options, one by one. What are the advantages? The disadvantages? Usually, a pretty clear winner emerges—a solution that both you and your child can live with.

Empower your child to solve the problem.

5. Let your child face the consequences.

Remember those times in your life when you had no choice but to face the music? You'd done something you shouldn't have—or not done something that was expected of you. You probably still cringe thinking about one of your actions. But you learned. You learned that you didn't like the feeling and the consequences that went along with messing up. And eventually you decided not to do that ever again. All on your own.

This may come as a big surprise to conscientious parents, but letting your child face the consequences of his actions or nonactions can be a gift to him *and* to you.

If your child doesn't finish his homework, is late returning his library books, or doesn't get home in time for dinner, those are *his* problems.

He'll need to deal with the teacher the next day, pay a fine before he can take out more books, and either fix himself something to eat or go to bed hungry—none of which are life-threatening and all of which are uncomfortable enough to cause him to think.

On the other hand, if your nine-year-old leaves streaks of peanut butter and globs of strawberry jelly, open cereal boxes, bread crumbs, half-empty milk glasses, and various scuzzy utensils all over the kitchen counter, the situation is a little different. It now becomes *your* problem, with no immediate natural consequences to your child. So you need to create some consequences—such as not starting dinner until the kitchen is cleaned.

Just be aware of whose life is going to be impacted by your child's actions. If it's his life alone (and no real harm can come to him), let him face the consequences. If your life is affected by his behavior, then create the consequences for him.

Let your child face the consequences.

**FIVE STEPS TO HELP
YOUR CHILD BECOME
INDEPENDENT AND
RESPONSIBLE**

- Actively listen to your child
- Tell your child out loud that you care
- Admit to your child that you can't solve the problem alone
- Empower your child to solve the problem
- Let your child face the consequences

FIVE STEPS TO HELP YOUR CHILD BECOME INDEPENDENT AND RESPONSIBLE

✓ ACTIVELY LISTEN TO YOUR CHILD

✓ TELL YOUR CHILD OUT LOUD THAT YOU CARE

✓ ADMIT TO YOUR CHILD THAT YOU CAN'T SOLVE THE PROBLEM ALONE

✓ EMPOWER YOUR CHILD TO SOLVE THE PROBLEM

✓ LET YOUR CHILD FACE THE CONSEQUENCES

Dispense ad lib _____ Carolyn Ann Meeks _____ M.D.

Part III • FEELING GOOD

8 • Five Steps to Increase Your Self-Esteem

Nearly every parent who has come to me for counseling has wanted his or her child to grow up confident and self-assured, filled with the kind of regard for himself, his potentials, and his needs that allows him to become a happy, self-reliant, fulfilled adult. If you want to improve your child's self-esteem, the very best way to do that is to find out how to improve your own self-esteem.

By role modeling the kind of positive attitude and behavior you want your child to have, you stand a much greater chance of having your child develop the same attitude and behavior. When you truly feel good about yourself, you will find that you will be more patient, more creative, more naturally communicative, and more enthusiastic about life in general.

In this chapter you'll find five sure-fire ways of increasing your own self-esteem. You will be happier, your child will be happier, and you will be setting an example for your child that will help him grow into an effective, affirming, and confident adult.

1. Use positive self-talk.

Every waking moment we are programming our minds. Don't believe me? Take a few minutes right now and tune into all the chatter going on in your head. "I'm hungry. What time is it anyway? Only eleven. Too early for lunch. But I'm hungry. If I eat lunch now I'll be hungry again at three. Wonder what's in the fridge. I want something sweet. Cheesecake, a Hershey bar, a can of chocolate syrup, a gallon of ice cream, fourteen pounds of M&M's. There I go, out of control. I'm fat as a pig already. Can't control anything in my life . . ."

The fact that you wait until noon and have a tuna sandwich without a speck of chocolate on it, and that you wear a size 8 dress is of no consequence to your mind, which has now been programmed with negative thoughts: My eating is out of control; I'm fat as a pig; I can't control anything in my life.

It doesn't take any effort at all to program our minds negatively. We've been doing it all our lives. It does take an effort—at least in the beginning—to affirm the good we are, the good we want and the good we deserve. But it's well worth the effort!

Affirmations are positive statements. If we make affirmations to ourselves about ourselves, they take the place of the negative statements we've been feeding ourselves since we were young. They can be powerful expressions of our commitment to change.

Affirmations will work for you, if you'll give them a try.

Following is a list of positive statements my clients and workshop participants have found helpful. Choose the ones that are particularly meaningful for you, or make up your own. Write or say each one fifteen times a day. Try saying them with meaning and purpose, no matter how silly you feel. After a while, the affirmations will begin to "sink in" and become more a part of you.

Use positive self-talk.

The affirmations are repeated at the end of the book. Cut them out and put them on the dashboard of your car, on your bathroom mirror, on the refrigerator, on your wallet—wherever you're sure not to miss them.

Keep this up for seven days and observe the difference it makes in your life!

AFFIRMATIONS

I, _____, am a competent and lovable mom/dad, and I deserve to respect myself and have others respect me.

I, _____, love being a parent, and I find new ways to enjoy it every day.

I, _____, am having fun with what I am doing right now.

I, _____, am willing to let abundant good flow into my life.

I, _____, am honest with myself about what is really important to me, as opposed to what is of value to those around me.

I, _____, am excited by all the possibilities in my life.

I, _____, am willing to have more and more (fun, peace, relaxation, joy, money, time with my kids, time alone, etc.) in my life.

I, _____, care enough about my children to set limits.

I, _____, now open myself to receive the love of others.

I, _____, now see my children as the wondrous, unique, delightful beings that they are, and I am willing to show them how much I appreciate them.

2. Get rid of your "shoulds."

"Oh, I really should be getting home—I should be there when the kids get home. They can't seem to remember to take their key. I guess I should put a note on their lunch bags to remind them." Sound familiar?

We grew up hearing it from our parents, and they grew up hearing it from theirs. Cave parents probably started it all by telling themselves they shouldn't spend so much time hunting for bear and should spend more time around the fire with their cave kids.

"In order to be a good parent, a worthwhile person, I *should* do this and I *shouldn't* do that." Inference: There's some invisible something out there that writes the rules and judges me on whether or not I follow them. I'm not in charge.

Here's a way out of the "should" trap:

Take one minute right now and do the following exercise. Do it as fast as you can, without giving too much thought to what you write. In the space below, write three "should" sentences that relate to your life (e.g., "I should keep the house cleaner"; "I should call my mother"; "I should go on a diet").

1. _____

2. _____

3. _____

Now go back over your three sentences and replace the "shoulds" with "choose to" or "choose not to," whichever one is the truth for you right now.

"I choose to go home now because I want to be there when my kids get home," puts the control back where it belongs—with *you*.

Taking control of your own life is one of the most important steps in building self-esteem.

3. Take your passion—make it happen!

What is it that really excites you? If you could do *anything*—if you had all the courage, education, money, and support you needed to accomplish whatever you wanted—what would you do? What do you really *want* out of life? These may be the most important questions you'll ever ask yourself. The answers are what will get you in touch with your passion—that part of you that comes alive with enthusiasm and energy, the part that makes life worth living. What are *your* dreams? Is there something you have been putting off that you could begin *now*? Make a list of short-term and long-term goals for you:

SHORT-TERM GOALS:

1. _____

2. _____

LONG-TERM GOALS:

1. _____

2. _____

3. _____   3. _____

4. _____   4. _____

5. _____   5. _____

Spend time with this. Really give it some thought. And when you've come up with answers, ask yourself this: "Why am I not doing it?" Chances are, the reason is fear.

A way to walk through fear is to list the "pros" and "cons" of doing whatever it is that "turns on" the "juice" for you. Then, for every "con" list all the ways you could overcome that barrier.

GOAL: _____

PROS   **CONS**   **WAYS TO OVERCOME**

_____   _____   _____

_____   _____   _____

_____   _____   _____

_____   _____   _____

_____   _____   _____

Then go for it! Remember, life is not a dress rehearsal.

4. Consider taking an assertiveness training class.

Some parents have mastered good assertiveness skills from an early age. If this is the case for you, then skip ahead to the next point. But if assertiveness does not come easily to you, read on.

Assertiveness does not mean trampling all over everyone else's feelings while saying "ME FIRST!" It *does* mean asking for what you want in a nonhurtful way.

Ten years ago, when I took an assertiveness training class, my sister was afraid I might learn how to be rude and embarrass her in a restaurant—shout out something like, "Hey, waiter, you forgot to put the nuts on my hot fudge sundae!" But instead, I learned a better way: "Excuse me, but I would *love* to have some nuts on my sundae." I found that a waiter would run, not walk, to assist me. Occasionally you may have to be aggressive to deal with major problems, and it's important to know how to do that.

Take your passion—make it happen.

I recommend taking an assertiveness training class. They are frequently offered by church and community organizations.

If you can enhance your assertiveness skills, you can role model them to your child. You will find that assertiveness directly improves your parenting effectiveness.

Consider taking an assertiveness training class.

5. Remember, it's never too late to have a happy childhood.

Our self-esteem results from messages we received as children, usually before the age of five. If you're like most of us, you received mixed messages. Some were positive, some were negative.

But no matter how negative the messages were, it's never too late to change them!

When I was a little girl, I wanted a Toni doll that could be given a home permanent. I wanted one for my birthday. I wanted one for Christmas. I wanted one for Easter and Valentine's Day and St. Patrick's Day and every other occasion that warranted a gift. But I never got one.

That Toni doll became a symbol to me that said, "I never get what I want."

Years later, when I was going through a particularly difficult time and once again feeling that things never turned out the way I wanted, I remembered the Toni doll. But this time, instead of bemoaning the fact that no one ever gave me one, I went out and bought a beautiful doll for myself. For me the doll symbolized that "I have learned to take care of my wants and needs."

Create the environment *now* you wish you had as a child. Tell yourself *now* the things you wish your parents had told you when you were young. Decide what kind of person you want to be—not what kind of person your parents told you you were—and start telling yourself that's who you are *now*.

It's never too late to modify your behavior, your environment, your choices. Just remember, the more good you allow into your life, the more good can flow out. If your cup is empty, you have nothing to give to others, but if it is full to overflowing, everyone benefits. You will find that the better you feel about yourself in general, the more confident and skillful you will be as a parent.

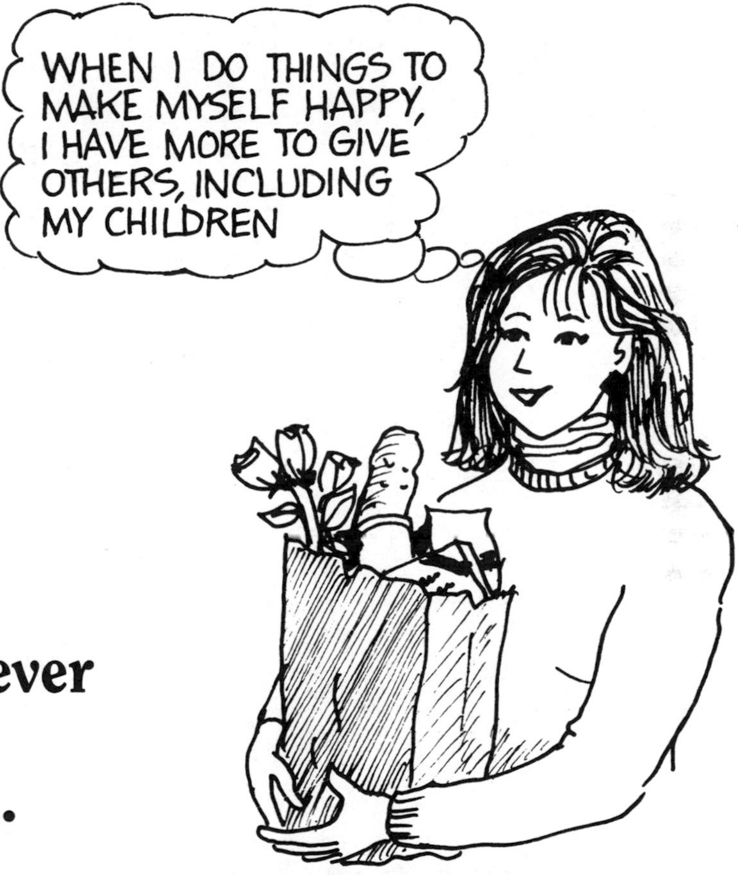

Remember: it's never too late to have a happy childhood.

FIVE STEPS TO INCREASE YOUR SELF-ESTEEM

- Use positive self-talk
- Get rid of your "shoulds"
- Take your passion—make it happen
- Consider taking an assertiveness-training class
- Remember, it's never too late to have a happy childhood

 FIVE STEPS TO INCREASE YOUR SELF-ESTEEM

✓ USE POSITIVE SELF-TALK
✓ GET RID OF YOUR "SHOULDS"
✓ TAKE YOUR PASSION...MAKE IT HAPPEN
✓ CONSIDER TAKING AN ASSERTIVENESS TRAINING CLASS
✓ REMEMBER, IT'S NEVER TOO LATE TO HAVE A HAPPY CHILDHOOD

 Dispense ad lib _____ *Carolyn Ann Meeks* _____ M.D.

9 • Five Steps to Increase Your Child's Self-Esteem

Children with high self-esteem always behave better than children with low self-esteem. A seriously misbehaving child is a discouraged child—a child whose sense of self-worth needs a hefty boost. I have recommended the next five steps to parents in my practice, and they have never failed to bring about positive results. They require a real commitment on your part, but they are well worth the effort. These steps followed in sequence will lay a strong foundation in producing any desired improvement in your child's behavior.

1. List your child's positive strengths.

Take one minute right now to list every strength you can think of that your child has—everything you like about her. They don't have to be in any particular order—just put them all down. For example:

What I like about Jennifer:

She's—cute
—bright
—likes animals
—energetic
—creative

If you can't think of everything right now, start a list and add to it. Leave this list where you can see it in order to remember some of your child's strong points.

A lot of times we get so hooked into what our child is doing that's "wrong," "bad," or "not up to our standards," that we forget all about the delightful, endearing, thoughtful, creative, funny, loving, kind, clever things she does. The list will help you put things back in perspective, and help your child start seeing herself in a more balanced light.

List your child's positive strengths.

2. Radiate positive thoughts toward your child.

If you have a child whose behavior is a problem or a child whose self-esteem needs a real boost, try this:

For one week, every fifteen minutes your child is awake, give her a positive message either verbally or with body language. To remember to do this takes an enormous amount of motivation on your part. You could even leave Post-it notes or stickers on the refrigerator, phone, mirror, in lunch boxes, on her pillow—you get the idea. If you stick with it, you'll find the results will be transforming—for your child and for you.

Positive reinforcement can be things like a smile, thinking about her positive traits, saying "good job" if it applies, noticing when she's "right on," a pat on the back, a pat on the head, a hug, describing or acknowledging what she's doing, being glad your child is alive. You don't have to interrupt her playing in order to do this. You can simply radiate positive energy toward your child. She'll get the message whether it's said verbally or not. Children are very intuitive. They sense how you perceive them even when you don't verbalize it.

Radiate positive thoughts toward your child.

3. Give your child quality time.

If your child is misbehaving, being difficult, or causing you problems in some way, the last thing you probably want to do is spend time with him. But this is exactly when you need to do it.*

If your child is over ten, take him out to McDonald's or some other place he especially likes, for one-to-one time with you. No teaching, no questions, just time spent together talking about what he wants to talk about.

If you have a misbehaving child who is younger, try the following suggestion. It requires a real commitment on your part, but it's guaranteed to work if you follow all of the ground rules below:

FOCUS TIME

• Give your child fifteen to twenty minutes of your undivided attention three to five times a week. Don't exceed this amount of time or the whole exercise could become a burden and you might decide not to follow through.

• Label this time with your child's name, e.g., "Allison's Focus Time."

• Let your child choose the activity although, ideally, it shouldn't be something you absolutely hate to do. With a much younger child, you may want to offer some choices or suggestions.

• Since Focus Time is meant to be stress-free, do not teach your child at this time.

*If you have other children at home who are not misbehaving, I suggest you take time with them also. If you have more than one parent at home, I suggest alternating parents, giving time to each child if possible.

Give your child quality time.

- Do not ask questions. (Questions are a form of teaching—for example, when you ask, "What color is that?" you put yourself in a teacher-student relationship with your child. This is a "one-up" position. You will want to make this time relaxing for both of you.)
- Do describe what your child is doing. This may seem boring to you, but your child will know she has your undivided attention. Do praise your child's actions if appropriate.

Remember much misbehavior is nothing more than an appeal for love, and your undivided attention is an expression of love that can make all the difference.

4. Be careful how you label your child.

A child comes into the world with no preconceived notions about who she is or what she's capable of. She learns to fill in the blanks—to discover an identity—from her parents and others. She will live up—or down—to the labels her parents give her.

If a crying infant is ignored, she will "hear" "I am not worthy of attention." If she is handled roughly, she will "hear" "I am not worthy of care and love." If a three-year-old is not allowed to make any of her own decisions, is overly protected, she will "hear" "I am incapable; the world is a dangerous place—I better be afraid."

If you tell a five-year-old, "You are the messiest child I ever saw!" enough times, she will be well on her way to becoming the messiest child you ever saw. And if you tell her brother, "You're so stupid! Can't you do anything right?" there may very well come a time when he can't do anything right.

Be careful how you label your child.

What you say to others within earshot of your children is just as important as what you say to them directly. Often it will have more impact because they think they weren't supposed to hear it.

If your daughter has a problem with shyness, let her overhear you on the phone saying, "Christy is making a real effort to be outgoing. Today at the store she walked right up to Mrs. Widget and said 'Hello!' " Or let your son hear you tell your spouse how he helped you in with the groceries and what a considerate person he's becoming.

It's never too late to help your child build faith in her abilities. Start today by giving her positive labels!

5. Acknowledge effort, interest, and thinking.

With a child who is a perfectionist or with a child whose self-esteem is low, direct praise in the form of compliments may be discounted. No matter what you compliment the child on, there will always be someone she can think of who's better, smarter, prettier.

Tell John how good he is at building things with Legos and he'll tell you he isn't. Tell Mindi how well she did in her soccer game and she'll tell you she didn't. In this situation, you can always say, "Well, that's my opinion anyway." This reinforces the child's right to an opinion and still has an impact on the child.

Sometimes a perfectionist child will constantly frustrate herself with unrealistic standards. No matter what she has accomplished, it is not quite good enough—or, once accomplished, the achievement is considered insignificant. A child with low self-esteem may not become excited about any of

Acknowledge effort, interest, and thinking.

her achievements or may have quit trying. With the child who is a perfectionist or whose self-esteem is low, you may want to downplay achievement as a primary goal, and instead acknowledge (1) effort, (2) interest, and (3) thinking. If a child is noticed for these things, her overall attitude, well-being, and productivity will almost automatically improve.

1. *Acknowledge effort.* Effort is a valuable goal in itself. If a person makes a real effort in life, she can probably accomplish anything she wants. "Boy, it looks like you put some effort into that Lego building—just look at all the detail!" Or, "You really put in a lot of effort on the soccer field—you were hustling!"

2. *Acknowledge interest.* Notice and encourage special interests. If your child has some particular activity that captures her interest, this will add to her overall enthusiasm for life and help combat depression. What is it that makes your child excited? Cars? Games? Friends? A particular sport? Music? Whatever it is, recognize it. "You seem to be really interested in building things"; "You seem to like dancing a lot." "You really seem to love your music."

If your child develops strong interests when she's younger, chances are she will be more productively occupied as a teenager and less likely to turn to drugs or undesirable behavior for excitement.

3. *Acknowledge thinking.* Finally, see your child as a good thinker or problem solver. Whenever she comes up with a possible solution to a problem, comment on what a good problem-solver she is. If she puts thought into a project or her schoolwork, acknowledge her for it. If your child sees herself as a person who is capable of using her brain, she will be better able to get herself out of life's difficult situations.

184

FIVE STEPS TO INCREASE YOUR CHILD'S SELF-ESTEEM

- List your child's positive strengths
- Radiate positive thoughts toward your child
- Give your child quality time
- Be careful how you label your child
- Acknowledge effort, interest, and thinking

FIVE STEPS TO INCREASE YOUR CHILD'S SELF-ESTEEM

✓ LIST YOUR CHILD'S POSITIVE STRENGTHS

✓ RADIATE POSITIVE THOUGHTS TOWARD YOUR CHILD

✓ GIVE YOUR CHILD QUALITY TIME

✓ BE CAREFUL HOW YOU LABEL YOUR CHILD

✓ ACKNOWLEDGE EFFORT, INTEREST AND THINKING

 Dispense ad lib _____ *Carolyn Ann Meeks* _____ M.D.

10 • Five More Ways to Increase Your Child's Self-Esteem

1. Encourage your child to identify and express his feelings.

A child with high self-esteem:

- Is in touch with his feelings
- Trusts his feelings
- Knows it's healthy to act consistent with how he feels—e.g., happy, sad, angry

Problems will arise if parents feel responsible for every emotion their children experience. If the child is angry, unhappy, or depressed, these moms and dads feel it's because they aren't doing a good job—that somehow they've failed as parents. Often, what happens in response is that the child learns to bury his real feelings because they're not acceptable to his parents. In later years, the end result is a person who is so out of touch with his own feelings that he really doesn't know what he feels—or a person who is superficially pleasant but filled with the kind of unexpressed emotions that can lead to all sorts of other problems.

To enhance your child's self-esteem and avoid future problems, I recommend the following:

- Acknowledge your child's feelings—whatever they might be—even if these feelings make you uncomfortable.
- If your child seems upset or sad, ask him how he feels, or acknowledge his feelings by saying, "You seem sad" or "You seem upset."
- Don't try to change his feelings. Instead, let him talk about his feelings.
- Allow your child to notice and identify his own feelings. If your child is happy, notice it! Acknowledge his joy and enthusiasm by saying, "You seem very happy about that," rather than "You make me proud." In this way, you can help your child learn to feel good from within—to learn to please himself rather than please you.
- If your child is angry, upset, or frustrated, allow him to express these feelings. These are sometimes difficult emotions for parents to deal with in a child—often because some moms and dads have a hard time dealing with these emotions in themselves. The feelings exist, whether you want him to feel that way or not. By telling him, "Do not get angry," or discounting his feelings with comments like, "You have no right to get angry," or "Don't make such a big deal out of it," you're teaching your child not to trust or to show his feelings.

Here are some affirmations you might want to use with your child:

- "You are a good problem-solver."
- "You can learn by your mistakes."
- "It's O.K. to be sad sometimes."

- "You can figure it out."
- "You can trust your feelings."
- "You can make new friends."

Encourage your child to identify and express his feelings.

2. Use a positive tone of voice.

Your tone of voice and facial expression can label your child just as quickly as the words you use. If the tone is sarcastic, annoyed, or upset, it implies that your child is not O.K. as far as you are concerned, no matter what the words you use are saying.

If you greet your child with appreciation, enthusiasm, and caring in your voice, even if all you say is a simple, "Hi, how was school today?" your child will hear, "My mom is glad to see me. She cares about me and is happy I'm home."

Children form ideas about what they think they deserve in life by how they're treated by their parents. If a parent does all the requisite things but does them with sarcasm or hostility in his voice, the child is going to remember what is implied.

If you're upset over something that has nothing to do with your child—a fight with your spouse or trouble at work, for instance—*it's a good idea to explain to your child that you're dealing with grown-up issues that have made you angry or sad or anxious. This way, your child won't assume that the edge in your voice is because of something he's done.*

3. Teach your child how to convert a complaint into a request.

Eleven-year-old Roger was a blamer. He was also a complainer, a criticizer, and a fault-finder. He found something wrong with just about everything and everyone. In short, Roger was not one of the world's fun people.

By the time his parents made an appointment to see me about their son, they were desperate.

Use a positive tone of voice.

191

"Our son is always finding someone to blame about something," Roger's dad said. "When he was little we thought he'd outgrow it, but, if anything, it seems to be getting worse. Nobody likes to be around a kid who's always criticizing and complaining."

I told Roger's parents a secret every psychologist knows—that the blamer/complainer who is so hard on others is usually equally hard on himself. When we see something we don't like in someone else, it's often because we don't like that very thing in ourselves.

Someone like Roger, with an exaggerated need to blame and criticize, probably has a negative image of himself.

A very important thing you can do for a child who tends to blame and complain is to teach him how to turn the blame into a request. For example, the next time Roger comes running into the house complaining that Daniel down the street took his baseball mitt and ruined it, instead of listening to forty-five minutes worth of all the times Daniel did dastardly deeds, Roger's parents could suggest he turn the blame into a request. "Please replace my mitt," is really all Roger has to say to Daniel.

When Roger complains that the house is so hot he can hardly breathe and he feels like he's going to pass out, his mom can remind him to turn the blame into a request. "Please turn the heat down" will do the trick.

Once a child has learned to request instead of complain, he has effectively turned the volume down on his own inner critic as well—that part of him that says he's not good enough or worthy enough or smart enough or cute enough.

For teens, the most effective way of all to make a request is to preface it by a statement of commitment. "You're my sister and I want us to get along. My request is that you not use my things without asking."

Affirm to your child that he can turn the complaint into a request and he can ask for what he wants.

Teach your child how to convert a complaint into a request.

4. Encourage healthy connectedness.

For a child to feel good about himself, his social needs (developing friendships, learning to relate to people in a healthy way, etc.) must be honored by his parents. Some parents get so caught up in seeing that their children do well academically that they forget a child's social needs are just as important as scholastics.

There are several ways these social needs can be met:

- Through family—parents, siblings, other relatives
- Through peers
- Through adult mentors or role models other than parents
- Through pets

By the time a child is three, parents need to provide opportunities for him to socialize with children near his own age and older children or adults other than the parents. This may require "importing" children for a few hours once or twice a week if the child is not in preschool.

By the time the child is in school, it becomes even more important that intimate friendships be allowed to form.

Team sports, day care facilities, church or temple groups, YMCA/YWCA, and other activities all offer opportunities for forming friendships. Parents who have close friends of their own provide a model that helps a child see the healthy give-and-take of friendship and the emotional connectedness that it brings.

Encourage healthy connectedness.

For teens, "hanging out" time is just as important as school time. Since teenagers do a lot of this on the telephone, you may want to encourage your son or daughter to earn enough money for his or her own phone—or allow significant phone time if the family is sharing a phone.

The most important thing to remember here is the need for your child to have the time and the opportunities to develop close personal relationships outside the immediate family—even if that means a little bit of orchestration on your part to see that your child gets to Little League practice, Girl Scout meetings, or birthday parties.

5. Encourage independent discovery.

One of the greatest joys of childhood is discovering something new. And one of the greatest feelings of accomplishment for a child comes when she's been able to figure something out for herself.

Occasionally parents, in their eagerness to help their child, end up depriving her of the important gifts of discovery and accomplishment by providing the answers. Instead of learning to be creative and courageous in her approach to life and its problems, the child who has not been allowed to find her own solutions feels ill-equipped to face life's challenges when they appear.

It's important for your child to know that it's O.K. to fail—that failure is a tool for learning and temporary setbacks are part of the game. Let her know you believe in her—that you know she is capable of dealing with her failures as well as her successes. Tell your child about the times you tried and failed and what you learned from the experience.

Encourage your child, but don't do it for her. When it's possible, be there with her during the discovery process, but don't deprive her of the joy and sense of accomplishment that comes with working it out for herself.

Encourage independent discovery.

FIVE MORE WAYS TO INCREASE YOUR CHILD'S SELF-ESTEEM

- Encourage your child to identify and express his feelings
- Use a positive tone of voice
- Teach your child how to convert a complaint into a request
- Encourage healthy connectedness, both inside and outside the family
- Encourage independent discovery

 R

FIVE MORE WAYS TO INCREASE YOUR CHILD'S SELF-ESTEEM

✓ ENCOURAGE YOUR CHILD TO IDENTIFY AND EXPRESS HIS FEELINGS

✓ USE A POSITIVE TONE OF VOICE

✓ TEACH YOUR CHILD HOW TO CONVERT A COMPLAINT INTO A REQUEST

✓ ENCOURAGE HEALTHY CONNECTEDNESS, BOTH INSIDE & OUTSIDE THE FAMILY

✓ ENCOURAGE INDEPENDENT DISCOVERY

 Dispense ad lib _____ *Carolyn Ann Meeks* _____ M.D.

11 • How to Deal with Guilt

Three-year-old Rachel's mom is having a party. She has spent the morning shampooing the highly impractical off-white living room carpet that came with her house. No sooner is she finished than her daughter toddles into the room carrying her lunch plate of SpaghettiOs.

"Get back in the kitchen this instant!" Mom screams angrily, visualizing her newly cleaned carpet splattered with tomato sauce and pasta pieces. The startled child drops the dish, and both parent and child watch with horror as the red sauce slowly seeps into the carpet.

"NOW LOOK WHAT YOU'VE DONE!" Mom shrieks, lunging for the child. "I SPENT THREE HOURS CLEANING THIS CARPET, AND JUST LOOK AT IT! HAVEN'T I TOLD YOU NEVER TO BRING FOOD INTO THE LIVING ROOM? YOU'RE SO CLUMSY!" she yells, shaking her daughter's shoulders emphatically.

The three-year-old runs crying from the room.

Once the mess has been cleaned up and Mom's anger has subsided, the self-incrimination begins.

"What's more important, this stupid carpet or my daughter?" she asks herself with remorse. "I can always clean the carpet, but who knows if I can undo the damage I just did to her. What kind of monster am I anyway? Oh God, I feel so guilty! I'll never be able to live with myself."

Of all the human emotions, nonproductive guilt is perhaps the most insidious and the most useless. It causes our thoughts to be focused on the past—on an action taken or a word spoken that no amount of reliving can change. And by condemning ourselves for being less than perfect in the past, we create an unproductive, unpleasant, and often paralyzing present.

Parenting is rife with opportunities for guilt. Few of us have the time, energy, or resources to do the kind of job we'd like to do as parents. When we fall short of our own unrealistic expectations of perfection, we beat ourselves up—often mercilessly—over our "failures."

But there is hope. While it's impossible to avoid making mistakes in the future, there *are* ways out of the energy-wasting, joy-zapping guilt trap that keep you a prisoner of the mistakes you've made in the past.

1. Correct the situation within realistic limits.

O.K., so you've done your best Monster Mother or Fearsome Father routine. Your child is in her room sobbing. You know you were wrong and the guilt is starting to build. What do you do next?

First, assess the damage—was it physical, psychological, or both?

Next, weigh the options for correcting the situation. You might want to make a list of the pros and cons for each option—the process of writing it out in a form like this is often very therapeutic.

OPTIONS FOR CORRECTING MISTAKE

OPTION 1: _____

ADVANTAGES: **DISADVANTAGES:**

_____   _____

_____   _____

_____   _____

_____   _____

203

Correct the situation within realistic limits.

Finally, talk to your child and admit your mistake.

In the case of the spilled SpaghettiOs, Rachel's mom was stressed about the party she was having. She wanted everything to be perfect. She had worked hard all morning and, in an instant, saw her efforts dissolve in a flash of flying pasta. She's upset and feeling guilty. What can she do now?

The effect on Rachel, in this instance, was more psychological than physical—although shaking a child is dangerous and can cause serious damage.

After both parent and child have had a chance to calm down, Rachel's mom needs to tell her daughter she's sorry she got so mad. She can explain that she was worried about grown-up problems and she overreacted. Children are intuitive and understand the spirit of the apology even if they don't understand all the words or what precipitated the outburst in the first place.

She can give her daughter a hug, offer to fix her some more SpaghettiOs, and sit with her while she eats.

If Mom feels she needs help handling the stresses in her life so she won't run the risk of taking it out on her child, she can contact Parents Anonymous (see number 5), enroll in a parenting class, or seek counseling.

2. Forgive yourself for not being perfect.

Loving, conscientious parents who can forgive their children, their spouses, and their friends all manner of transgressions and imperfections will often hold on fiercely to the guilt they feel each time they themselves fall short. These sensitive, concerned moms and dads simply refuse to forgive themselves for not being perfect parents. And the guilts pile up.

Each new day provides countless opportunities for experiencing more guilt. Maybe you're exhausted from a long day at work and a slow commute home. When you walk in the door your daughter asks you to help her with a school project that is due the next day. You overreact. You scream that you aren't in fifth grade, she is, and it's up to her to do her own school work, not try to get you to do it for her. You send her to her room and tell her not to come out until the project is done. After you've had a chance to rest and regroup, the guilt sets in.

Maybe you're wondering where the money is going to come from to get you to the end of the month when the twins say they want new bikes for their birthday. You fly into a snit, telling them they not only can't have bikes, but they can't even have a party—in fact, they'll be lucky just to get a card.

The guilt you feel about not being a better provider is now compounded by the guilt you feel for having reacted so angrily.

Maybe you have to spend four nights away from home at a conference in Minneapolis. Even though your husband, your mother, and your baby-sitter are there to look after the baby, you're sure he'll be warped forever by the separation. The guilt is overwhelming.

No matter how badly you feel you've blown it with your child, forgive yourself by realizing that you did the very best you could in that particular moment.

The only perfect human beings have already ascended. If you're still on this earth, it's because you, like the rest of us, have a few more things to learn. So relax, and welcome to the human race!

Note: If you feel the mistake you made was so "unforgivable" that you need to "pay for it," devise your own way to make amends. The most productive thing you could do for your child and yourself is to enroll in a parenting workshop or seek counseling. You could also do something to help other children in your community. There are dozens of groups and organizations in even the smallest town that need volunteers.

Forgive yourself for not being perfect.

3. Let go of the past and move on to the present.

If you're an accountant and you make a mistake in computing a column of figures, you merely correct the mistake and go on. If you're in your car and you turn left when you should have turned right, you double back and make the correct turn. If you pick up the phone and dial a wrong number, you hang up and dial the correct one.

Every secretary expects to make a typing error once in a while. And even the best cook knows there are going to be times when a sauce curdles or a soufflé falls. When mistakes like these are made in the course of a day, we don't wail and moan and beat our chest in despair—we merely correct them or compensate for them and move on.

Why then do we expect our parenting skills to be perfect, and when we discover they aren't, proceed to chastise ourselves without mercy—sometimes to the point of actually making ourselves ill?

No matter how serious the mistake you think you made might be, once it's over, it's over. Correct the mistake, do your best to forgive yourself and move on!

Now it's time for *action*.

Do something *new*. Do something *fun*. Go some place you've never gone before. Start taking better care of yourself so you'll be better able to handle stress as it comes up—join a spa, take a yoga class. Get together with friends (but not to talk about how guilty you feel!). *Start living your life today.*

Let go of the past and move on to the present.

4. Use affirmations in moving toward positive change.

Affirmations are miracle-working tools. Pick out a few from this list, or make up your own. Write them fifteen times a day for a week and say them whenever you can. Pin them up around the house and put them in your car. This is a wonderful way to replace the negative thoughts and self-judgments that holding onto guilt perpetuates.

I, _____, am now ready to let go of guilt, accepting that I did the best I could with this situation, given the circumstances at the time.

I, _____, now take the necessary steps to look for new and better ways to parent.

I, _____, forgive myself for not being perfect.

I, _____, forgive my child for not being perfect.

I, _____, now have the courage to say "I'm sorry."

I, _____, can guide my child without needing to control him.

I, _____, now let go of my need to control.

I, _____, now let go of my unrealistic expectations about myself and my child.

I, _____, am now free of all self-destructive thoughts.

I, _____, welcome joy and laughter into my life.

I, _____, now choose to experience peace instead of guilt.

I, _____, now set realistic goals for myself.

I, _____, am now ready to live in the present instead of the past.

Use affirmations in moving toward positive change.

5. Take a class, join a support group, and/or seek professional counseling.

There is a lot of help available to parents who feel their actions or words might be harming their children, or who feel they need special support and understanding in their role as parents. Nearly every community has a crisis center or a crisis hot line where you can get a list of all the resources available in your area for helping you work through the feelings that are causing you or your child distress.

Among the most helpful are:

- Parenting classes that are age-group specific
- Self-esteem workshops
- Communication workshops
- Assertiveness training workshops
- Support groups for:
    Parents of children from specific age groups
    Single parents
    Stepparents
    Parents of disabled children
    Divorcing parents
- Counseling services with sliding-fee scales—available through the Community Mental Health Services in most communities

Take a class, join a support group, and/or seek professional counseling.

If you are afraid of your anger with your children and want to find a support group in your community, the following organizations may be helpful:

- **Parents Anonymous National Office**
  6733 S. Sepulveda Blvd., Suite 270
  Los Angeles, CA 90045
  1-800-421-0353

- **National Domestic Violence Hotline**
  1-800-333-7233

The National Domestic Violence Hotline will also be able to direct you to Parents Anonymous groups in your area, as well as to other organizations, such as Friendly Visitors, who will come into your home and teach you how to parent.

Other organizations that offer services for parents and children include:

- YMCA/YWCA
- Community centers
- Churches and religious organizations

HOW TO DEAL WITH GUILT

- Correct the situation within realistic limits
- Forgive yourself for not being perfect
- Let go of the past and move on to the present
- Use affirmations in moving toward positive change
- Take a class, join a support group, and/or seek professional counseling

R HOW TO DEAL WITH GUILT

✓ CORRECT THE SITUATION WITHIN REALISTIC LIMITS

✓ FORGIVE YOURSELF FOR NOT BEING PERFECT

✓ LET GO OF THE PAST AND MOVE ON TO THE PRESENT

✓ USE AFFIRMATIONS IN MOVING TOWARD POSITIVE CHANGE

✓ TAKE A CLASS, JOIN A SUPPORT GROUP, AND/OR SEEK PROFESSIONAL COUNSELING

Dispense ad lib _____ *Carolyn Ann Meeks* _____ M.D.

12 • Five Ways to Happily Be a Family

1. Remember, Lighten up!

Inside every grown-up there is a spontaneous, uninhibited kid who remembers what it feels like to be joyful—a kid who still wants and needs to play. The only trouble is, somewhere along the way to becoming an adult, we got the idea that we had to ignore that urge—to deny it, to bury it. And by the time we had kids of our own, most of us were very good at controlling and being in control, but we'd forgotten what it was like to have fun.

One of the greatest gifts you can offer your children is the gift of being a happy parent, of seeing the humor in this thing called *life*. Bill Cosby is a master at this. One of the reasons he's so popular is because he gives us permission to laugh at ourselves and to have fun with parenting.

Lighten up!

Take a close look at your children when they're laughing and having a great time, even to the point of being rambunctious.

Without judging, without trying to control, see if you can get in touch with the pure silliness of the moment, with the uninhibited joy, the excitement and total absorption in the present that your children are experiencing. Try to breathe in some of their excitement and sense of delight. Let your children teach you how to be joyful!

2. Family meeting: removing obstacles to have fun.

All of us want more fun in our lives. It alleviates stress. It keeps us young. It makes life worth living. But how can you have fun if your six and eight-year-olds are in the next room beating each other senseless amidst terrorizing screams of pain, if your preteen is moping around in a state of perpetual despair because you won't let her date a fourteen-year-old who wears black leather everything, and your "significant other" is ready to pack them all off to boarding school in Tibet.

Clearly, you need help to get from being frantic to having fun.

The family meeting can be just the answer you're looking for. It's a positive, cooperative way to work out problems that come up whenever several individuals with different needs, different wants, and different temperaments live together in the same place. And it's a wonderful opportunity to plan fun events and activities for the family.

Here's how it works:

Purpose:
• Provides a forum for resolving problems as well as for planning fun activities.

Ground Rules:
- Everyone in the household over the age of three is included. All opinions are honored.
- Everyone needs to be present at the meeting. If one member of the family should leave or disrupt the meeting, he loses the opportunity for input.

Frequency and Timing:
- Have a regularly scheduled time for the meeting each week (for example, Wednesday at the end of dinner).

Topics and Format:
- During the week, keep a list of any problems or requests that need discussion, consideration, or arbitration. A good place for the list is on the refrigerator, where everyone will have access to it.
- You may want to begin the meeting with "Celebrations." Give everyone a chance to contribute something they're happy about—an "A" on a test, making a new friend, receiving a compliment, learning a new skill.
- You could also start the meeting with a discussion of the fun stuff—planning a weekend outing, special requests for dinner or dessert, plans for a movie night, talk about a vacation that's coming up.
- Then move into the problem areas; have each person state his concerns and comments about a particular situation. Hear everyone out. For example, if you introduce the problem of fighting, you might say, "I'm committed to having more peace in this family. Fighting doesn't belong in our home. As your parent, I care enough about you to help you find better ways to control your temper

Establish family meetings to resolve difficulties.

and resolve differences. I can't resolve this problem without you. What are some ways we can reduce or eliminate fighting?" If no ideas are forthcoming, you can give your children time to think about it. Then go around the table and let everyone offer a suggestion. Give your ideas, too.

Have someone write down all the suggestions that are made. For example:

Possible Solutions for Fighting:
    Send all fighting participants outside to resolve their differences. Nobody is allowed inside until the fighting has stopped.
    Send everyone who is fighting to their rooms.
    Everyone who fights has to put ten cents into a jackpot for "Mom's stress relief fund."
    Start a star chart for no fighting. As soon as there is a day with no fighting, order out for pizza to celebrate.

Consider any ideas that seem feasible or practical. Take a vote as to which solution to try. Problems are best resolved when offending parties are involved in the solution. Letting everyone have a say gives them a chance to ventilate their feelings; allowing everyone the opportunity to voice possible strategies for resolution adds to the likelihood of success when the suggestions are implemented. Whenever possible try to use your children's suggestions in the resolution.

3. Think fun!

The key to having fun, especially with children, is spontaneity and creativity. A friend of mine used to take her two sons on "adventures" when they were young. The adventures were never elaborate or expensive, but because they always came as a surprise, the children delighted in them. In fact, neighbor children used to ask if they could spend the night in the hope there would be an adventure during their stay.

One hot summer night, Mom woke her kids at eleven o'clock, hustled them into the car, and took them to the local Baskin-Robbins for ice cream. Another time, they [Seattle residents] took an early-morning ferry ride to a nearby island for breakfast. There was a "no-occasion" surprise party where ten of her sons' friends and a mountain of pizzas were waiting when the boys got home from soccer practice one afternoon. There were Saturdays when Mom said, "Let's forget the chores and have a picnic," and one steamy August morning everybody got up at four o'clock and went swimming before sunrise.

Let your imagination have free rein when planning activities both children and adults will enjoy. Here are some starters:

• Weekend treasure hunts that require some real ingenuity on the part of your kids and their friends.

• A visit to the local newspaper (many have tours), where your kids can watch the fascinating printing process.

• A trip to Mom or Dad's office for the morning (maybe even lunch out if they've been especially good).

Think fun and plan fun.

- A taffy pull—it's easy, it's fun, and it's yummy!
- Art projects—making papier-mâché masks for Halloween can be a wonderful project, or making valentines or bread-dough Christmas ornaments.
- Exercise and sports—jogging, walking, swimming, tennis, bowling, playing catch, throwing a Frisbee, bike rides. There are lots of important "causes" that have walk-a-thons during the spring and summer. Consider entering the whole family!
- Mini-vacations—day-long getaways to the beach, the mountains, or a pretty park nearby.
- Sleep-outs. If you have a back yard, a great summer experience is for the whole family to take sleeping bags and lie out under the stars. This is especially exciting during the late summer, when there are lots of shooting stars.
- Kitchen projects where neatness is no object—making cookies or candied apples or baking bread (children as young as four love this process)—anything that gets the kids totally involved.
- Nature hikes—there are endless possibilities here for fun and learning.
- Planting and caring for a garden—each child could have his own small plot, with a trip to the seed store, where he gets to pick out what he wants to grow.

As you can see, the possibilities are endless, and except for a few ingredients, none of those listed entails an expense. So enjoy yourselves and enjoy your children!

4. Make time for fun.

Before you can have fun with your children, you need to make the *time* to have fun with them. This may require some prioritizing on your part, which is actually a very simple process.

Every morning, make a list of the *six most important things* you want to accomplish that day. The list should include the things that will give you the greatest sense of satisfaction: going to work, time with your children, time with your partner, exercising, taking a bubble bath, shopping for groceries.

If there are things you think you "should" do but just don't feel like doing, don't want to do, or there simply isn't time, put them on a list of things you're *not* going to do that day: clean the garage, shop for Christmas, make everyone's lunch, do the laundry, clean the family room. You get the idea.

Give yourself a chance to be happy and satisfied with what you've done, and let go of the guilt around things you can't (or don't want to) get to that day.

By taking care of what is most important to you each day and forgetting about the rest, you can start letting go of the idea that you need to be Superman or Wonder Woman, accomplishing herculean tasks that only leave you feeling frazzled, exhausted, and guilty. And you can start building in time for *fun*!

Make time for fun.

5. Celebrate each new day!

Every single day there is something to celebrate. It doesn't have to be something big like a birthday or a raise or an anniversary. It can be something as simple as just making it through the day. Maybe your child got ready for bed when you asked him to, or you had a peaceful dinner. Maybe you got a pay check, or you found out you don't need a new roof after all. Maybe you saw the first crocus of spring, or everybody in the family was well at the same time. There are lots of reasons to be grateful, lots of reasons to celebrate.

Celebrate each new day.

FIVE WAYS TO HAPPILY BE A FAMILY

- Lighten up!
- Establish family meetings to resolve difficulties
- Think and plan fun!
- Make time for fun
- Celebrate each new day!

CAROLYN ANN MEEKS M.D. ● Prescriptions for Parenting

 FIVE WAYS TO HAPPILY BE A FAMILY

✓ LIGHTEN UP!

✓ ESTABLISH FAMILY MEETINGS TO RESOLVE DIFFICULTIES

✓ THINK AND PLAN FUN!

✓ MAKE TIME FOR FUN

✓ CELEBRATE EACH NEW DAY!

 Dispense ad lib _____ Carolyn Ann Meeks _____ M.D.

Recommended Reading

Brazelton, T. Berry. *Toddlers and Parents*. New York: Dell Publishing, 1989.

Brazelton, T. Berry. *To Listen to a Child*. Reading, Mass.: Addison-Wesley, 1984.

Briggs, Dorothy Corkille. *Your Child's Self-Esteem*. New York: Dolphin Books, Doubleday, 1975.

Clarke, Jean Illsley. *Self-Esteem: A Family Affair*. New York: Harper & Row, 1980.

Clarke, Jean Illsley, et al. *Help! for Parents* Vol. 1–6. San Francisco: Harper & Row, 1986.

Cosby, Bill. *Fatherhood*. New York: Berkley Publishing, 1987.

Crary, Elizabeth. *Without Spanking or Spoiling*. Seattle, Wash.: Parenting Press, 1979.

Dinkmeyer, Don, and McKay, Gary D. *The Parent's Handbook: Systematic Training for Effective Parenting (STEP)*. New York: Random House, 1982.

Faber, Adele, and Mazlish, Elaine. *How to Talk So Kids Will Listen & Listen So Kids Will Talk*. New York: Avon Books, 1980.

Jampolsky, Gerald G., M.D. *Love Is Letting Go of Fear*. New York: Bantam Books, 1982.

Neifert, Marianne, M.D.; Price, Anne; and Dana, Nancy. *Dr. Mom*. New York: New American Library, 1986.

Spock, Benjamin, M.D., and Rothenberg, Michael B., M.D. *Dr. Spock's Baby and Child Care*. New York: Pocket Books, 1985.

Weinhaus, Evonne, and Friedman, Karen. *Stop Struggling with Your Teen*. New York: Penguin Books, 1988.

Appendix

Affirmations for Parents

Affirmations can be powerful expressions of commitment to change. Use these positive thoughts to replace self-doubt and self-criticism. Take your favorite affirmations from the following list. Write or say these affirmations fifteen times a day for four days. The affirmations will become a part of you in a very powerful and positive way.

I, _____, am a competent and lovable mom/dad, and I deserve to respect myself and have others respect me.

I, _____, am having fun with what I am doing right now.

I, _____, love being a parent, and I find new ways to enjoy it every day.

I, _____, am willing to let abundant good flow into my life.

I, _____, am honest with myself about what is really important to me, as opposed to what is of value to those around me.

I, _____, care enough about my children to set limits.

I, _____, am excited by all the possibilities in my life.

I, _____, now open myself to receive the love of others.

I, _____, am willing to have more and more (fun, peace, relaxation, joy, money, time with my kids, time alone, etc.) in my life.

I, _____, now see my children as the wondrous, unique, delightful beings that they are, and I am willing to show them how much I appreciate them.

I, _____, am ready to let go of guilt, knowing I did the best I could with this situation, given the circumstances at the time.

I, _____, forgive my child for not being perfect.

I, _____, now take the necessary steps to look for new and better ways to parent.

I, _____, now have the courage to say "I'm sorry."

I, _____, forgive myself for not being perfect.

I, _____, can guide my child without needing to control him.

I, _____, now let go of my need to control.

I, _____, welcome joy and laughter into my life.

I, _____, now let go of my unrealistic expectations about myself and my child.

I, _____, now choose to experience peace instead of guilt.

I, _____, am now free of all self-destructive thoughts.

I, _____, now set realistic goals for myself.

I, _____, am now ready to live in the present instead of the past.

I, _____, can deal constructively with my child's misbehavior when it occurs.

Affirmations You Can Say to Your Child

Here are some positive thoughts that you can say or give to your child. Feel free to adopt them or to create new ones especially for your child.

You are a good problem solver.	You can learn by your mistakes.
It's O.K. to be sad sometimes.	You can make new friends.

You can figure it out.	You can ask for what you want.
You can trust your feelings.	You can turn a complaint into a request.

I'm so glad you're in my life.

The world is a better place because you're here.

I'm so glad you're you.

I love you just the way you are.